Relationship Cookbook

Anthony C. Rucker

G Publishing LLC

Detroit   Los Angeles   Atlanta

Published by G Publishing LLC
800.478.2691
www.gpublishingsuccess.com
In association with
Rucker Media Group Publishing
Rucker Media Group, LLC.
5482 Wilshire Blvd, Suite #1529
Los Angeles, CA 90036
917.376.7876
www.ruckermedia.com

©2005, 2006, 2007 Anthony C. Rucker, aka Da Boogie Man
All rights reserved
Printed in the USA. First Edition.

LIBRARY OF CONGRESS
CATALOGING-IN-PUBLICATION DATA
Rucker, Anthony.
      Relationship Cookbook.
        I. Family and Relationships: Love and Romance
        II. Self-Help
        III. Body, Mind & Spirit

Library of Congress Control Number: 2007939380
ISBN 13: 978-0-9796978-8-3
     10: 0-9796978-8-3

The author is available for lectures, workshops and other speaking engagements. Contact bookings@relationshipcook.com 718.598.7491 or 5482 Wilshire Blvd, Suite #1529, Los Angeles, CA 90036

Book Layout & Design by Marléna Gasper Rucker for Rucker Media Group
Cover Photograph by Shawn King for King Photography

Praise for the *Relationship* Cookbook

"Straightforward and truthful." – Cherise Davis, Senior Editor, Simon & Schuster

"Relationship Cookbook didactically shifts one's way of thinking toward a more harmonic union with one's mate."
 – Bruce George, Co-Founder of Def Poetry Jam

"…Ingenious concept. You're taking Dr. Phil's job for sure."
– Samona, Director of Cocoa Singles

"I've never thought about it like that before. . ." – D. Austin, Graphic Designer, Single

"I wish I had this book before I filed for divorce." – Tamika Hayes

*This is dedicated to my
lovely & perfect wife.
You are the fulfillment of the highest
relationship & sweetest joy I know.
Being with you is proof
that God loves me.*

Author's Note

    Greetings, I'm glad that you started this journey with me. The health and well being of relationships are very important to me because they not only shape our personal lives but also the world we live in. I love happiness and love to see people who are happy. Anything I can do to aid and add to this happiness is not only my joy it is my obligation.

    Through my life I've watched people subscribe to philosophies and stereotypes about one another that drew us further and further apart. I could never understand how we continued to use ideas and concepts that have never worked for us and probably never will. I longed for other choices. All I could think is that there has to be a different way to interact with each other that is more beneficial than the way we interact now.

What I found was nothing new. It wasn't an epiphany that was never seen before. What I found was at the heart and root of what and who we are as human beings. I found that the simplicity of loving and being true to oneself and extending that courtesy to others is the foundation of all happiness and fulfilling relationships.

You will not find sections on abuse or infidelity or lying spouses or emotional cruelty or disrespect or neglect. Those acts are not a part of relationships. Just like burning food is not a part of cooking. Besides we know that the best way not to burn food is to create good cooking habits. The aforementioned negative aspects of our lives are dysfunctional acts that we carry out when we are out of balance and integrity, and I think we need to know in depth how to prepare and build great relationships before we can truly understand how to address actions that destroy them. With that in mind make sure to pay close attention to the "special ingredient" boxes and headlines in the various sections, they will contain summaries and explanations of key points to help make the content of the book easier to understand.

This book draws the correlation between cooking and the simplicity of loving. It also offers a perspective of relationships that you've never considered that provides a clearer understanding of the concept and process of loving wholly and freely. Some may label this a self-help book. I call it a book of advice. In the end we are not helped until we help ourselves. What enlightens us or brings us to a point where we desire to help ourselves, I call good advice. So I offer you my advice. I hope this will inspire us all to create or recreate our relationships into healthy experiences full of flavor and life.

My hope for us all is a world where we experience the best and most wonderful parts of each other each and every day.

Table of Contents

Introduction 15
- Relationship Doom?! 23

PreCooking 27
- Preparation Before Cooking 34
- Deciding. Budgeting. Shopping 35
- Removing "You" from the Situation 43
- How to Clean Your Kitchen 46
- Relationship Myths 53
- The Proper Cooking Utensils 78
- Pots & Pans 81
- Conventional Ovens vs. Microwaves 98

Cooking 113
- Unwrapping & Inspecting 116
- Eating Undercooked Food 121
- Cooking 126
- Simmering 131
- Seasoning 133
- Dipping in the Pot: Playing Married 134
- Playing With Knives 142
- Setting the Table 155

Eating 157
- Talking With Your Mouth Full 160
- Fresh vs. Spoiled Food 165
- Clean Up When You're Done 171

Acknowledgements 173
- Index 174
- Other Books by Da Boogie Man 176

*Eat for health & taste.
Enjoy life, love freely...*

What is the relationship cookbook? It's really simple. The relationship cookbook is a book of perspectives and associations that I believe will help you better understand, navigate, and nurture relationships. To further clarify that answer though, we need to go back some years.

When I went to college I was introduced to the idea of being the working poor. I was working my behind off and was always broke. I thought of getting a job, but being a computer science major and math major left very little time for me to do so. Like a great deal of working students, I could have made time for a job, sacrificed sleep and peace of mind and struggled through. However, I was always taught to work smarter not harder. So I had to come up with another solution.

I thought about working for UPS. It was only four hours a day, I thought, it couldn't be that hard. There I was on my first day of work, in the back of a truck lifting heavy boxes for four hours. After I was done I only had energy enough to find a bed a pillow and hard sleep. At that point I knew there had to be a better way to bring money into my lint filled pockets. The light came on.

Since high school I had helped peers with homework and studying for exams. In college there are the walking-lost; those who have no idea what their professors are talking about and absolutely no idea what to do to secure a decent grade from them. I started making the connection that I made when I used to shovel drive ways and mow lawns; people will pay you to do work that they don't want to do or don't have time to do. CHA-CHING!!

All I had to do was charge for the tutoring I was doing and presto-change-o I go from hungry to full, in the time it takes to solve a math equation, write a paper, or write a computer program. Considering how important college grades are, getting students to pay for them wouldn't be that hard.

I let everyone know that I was no longer a tutor to just friends, now I was a brain for hire. If you had money we were now "friends." The next thing you know I am working with students who are as lost as a cat at a dog show. Alas, a new problem; if customers paid money for help they wanted results. I couldn't just say "You're hopeless. Either cheat or be prepared to bomb." I found that results from frustrated, broke, overworked, over partied college students don't come easy and take a whole lot of time, which took away from the time I needed to do my work and enjoy the benefits of being a single man on a college campus. There were times I hid from the student center because I had so many friends who needed to be tutored that I would have had to skip all of my classes to meet with them.

At that point I decided I needed a process of tutoring that would cut time and still be effective. The only problem was I didn't have one. Until one day one of my friends opened my eyes to what I needed to do.

He was in calculus and couldn't catch the concepts of anything. Derivatives, integrals, series, everything seemed to float into the land of "blah, blah, blah" when it went into his ears. But he loved to eat, I mean loved to eat. So playing around I asked him what his favorite foods were. Then I began to call all the different components by the foods he liked. Exponents became doughnuts, variables became bacon, derivatives became shopping. Pretty soon calculus was a meal. When it came to the different symbols and theories I created a sort of math-to-English dictionary to help him translate them. When you see this say that, when you read that say this. A perfect match if there ever was one.

By the time we were finished he was getting problems right that he hadn't figured out in weeks. I wasn't sure how or why this worked but I liked it. It exponentially increased his understanding and retention and cut the amount of time I needed to tutor him. The perfect combination needed to ensure that I make enough money to eat, retain business, and make it to classes.

The trick now was to figure out what I had done so I could do it again for all the other subjects I tutored. After some careful contemplation I came to the conclusion that most of us are intimidated by subject matter they don't know, but if you can dress them in something familiar and easy to recognize, it would take away their apprehension and alleviate a large amount of their fear. And if by some chance they started to have fun it would improve their learning curve. The challenge became finding a way to properly associate what they were familiar with to the subjects they were struggling through. Doughnuts and bacon will only take you so far. In my journey, I've used everything from love, to houses, to lawns, to CDs, to boyfriends and girlfriends, all depending on the frame of reference most comfortable to whomever I was dealing with.

A strange trend began happening. Everybody I tutored improved their grades. Not some, not a few, not a lot, every one improved to a B or better. I then ran into the same problem I had before-more students who wanted tutoring than I could handle. Because of my success, I now faced a different problem. How do I teach others to do what I do to take some of the pressure off of me? I began to formulate a philosophy and process to what I was doing. It was necessary to develop some form of methodology to this system if I was going to teach it to someone else; however, it never manifested. I just considered myself some sort of freak of nature doomed to hiding from confused students forever, which is exactly what I did for most of my college career.

Oddly enough, after college my understanding began to become clearer. It happened in the form of a friend. You know the friend everyone has who seems to know everything and more about you than you. That's him! In one of our many conversations we began talking about methods of teaching, western vs. eastern philosophies, and how that related to our "teaching" methods. He then gave me the basis of my own understanding. It wasn't so much that I dealt with subject matter that was familiar to them. It was that I dealt with tangible concrete everyday happenings that were easier to understand and process. After all, math and science are full of concepts. Concepts are abstract and harder to grasp, so by taking everyday happenings and relating them to complex ideas the ideas became easier to understand. BINGO! That's it! It's about a million years too late to use but nevertheless its here.

It all made sense. He said, "Yeah, we teach backwards. We need to teach about things we can touch before we teach about things we can't. It makes learning easier." I know it worked for me. He was preaching to the choir. Almost prophetically he followed with, "You ought to write a book about how to teach math, it would kill." I, sad to say, was all mathed-out. I tutored so much in my life that I wanted nothing else to do with it. I then realized that there's more to life than math.

What I was most interested in was our relationships to one another. If I wrote a book about anything, I would want it to be about that. But who am I to be writing a book about relationships? I've given advice to friends and received great advice from married couples who are twenty, thirty, and fifty years married, in love and happy, but does that qualify me to write a book on relationships? And if I do write a book what will I use as a point of reference?

The first revelation I came to was that relationships are not an exact science or else we wouldn't have such problems with them. The second was that people who are considered "experts" weren't right all the time, just right more than most. Thirdly, it was evident that if experts had all the answers we wouldn't still be looking for them, the answers that is. The conclusion then came kind of easy; the help I've extended to family and friends I could extend to everybody else and they can take it for what it's worth. The knowledge I've acquired has done me well and therefore might do the same for others. I've been the person friends have come to for years for advice about a little of everything. The only difference now is that I would be dealing with a bigger audience. Thinking of it like that made it look "not so big" and very doable. It was decided, I was going to write a book on relationships. Now the question became, how do I do it?

Let's not rebuild the wheel, was my first thought. *What have I used to give advice in the past?*, was the second. That was simple, food! No matter what the topic food always found a way to make sense. Why not? Everybody eats food. Everybody likes food. I'll write a book about relationships and call it "The Relationship Cookbook." Now the answer to my very first question is clear. The relationship cookbook is a book of perspectives and associations that I believe will help you better understand, navigate, and nurture relationships.

Our perspectives shape our reality and most of our perspectives are full of generalizations, stereotypes, and prejudices. To be truthful, we have generalized ourselves into nausea and in most cases we think we are dealing with concepts and ideas instead of with people.

We talk about life, circumstances, infidelity, destiny and true love. What we are really talking about is how we live our lives and how that living affects us. Instead of admitting we're dealing with each other, we've created a gray area that allows us to excuse ourselves from responsibility and truth.

The gray area is where no one is responsible for their actions and no one is held accountable for anything they do. If you allow yourself to be used, it's love's fault. If someone hurts you, you blame it on immaturity and infidelity. If we can't get a date we blame it superficiality, mass media, shallowness, or a shortage of good mates. The aforementioned reasons are all projections to divert responsibility and guilt from the true culprits – us. We are the cause and effect of everything in our lives. You show me where you were victimized by a state of mind, way of thinking, or circumstance of life and I'll show you a person who was responsible; but admitting we mess up our own lives is uncomfortable, unpopular, and painful, so we create the gray area to avoid the discomfort and pain and to live in a mythical space where we are always justified all the time.

In this area we lose track of ourselves and those we love. That's where this book comes in. It offers advice and instruction that is concrete and tangible, as a reference point to how we relate to and with each other.

Through the art of cooking we will explore this maddening universe of emotion and relationships and make some sense of it.

Relationship Doom?!

Are relationships really complex, hopeless, doomed to failure, and predisposed to conflict? Of course not. Relationships are almost exactly like our vision. If persons or places are too far away we can't tell what we are looking at, but as we get closer we can begin to notice details and specifics and make sense of what we are seeing. If we get too close we lose focus and full view of where we are and what we're looking at. Sounds simple doesn't it. If we are too distant from someone, we really don't know who or what they are. If we're too close, we lose focus on whom and what they are and their purposes in our lives.

It's not a coincidence that principles in our lives overlap, and that our senses and ecosystem can teach us how to better understand ourselves. In an attempt to make us and our situations bigger than they are, we have leveled a measure of importance on certain emotions in regards to relationships. In doing so we have also assumed that different rules, judgments, and processes apply to those emotions than the ones that rule our everyday lives. Living by two separate sets of emotional rules is where we have caused ourselves the most pain. Not saying good judgment can totally alleviate pain from our relationships, but it definitely can minimize it and change the nature of it.

In looking at the magnitude and importance of relationships to ourselves, we have not honestly measured the importance of the relationships to our partners/significant others. Just because we value the relationship it doesn't mean our partners do. Just because we are willing to sacrifice everything to salvage the relationship it doesn't mean our partners will. In important situations we act out of balance, assuming this behavior is okay because of the situation. As implied with balance, where there is none, one will fall over. We need to find a balance in distance that allows us to enjoy what we are seeing without losing focus of it. It is our actions that create imbalance that distort our perspectives. Removing these habits and practicing being balanced will help us to habitually keep our relationships is focus.

Is this analogy oversimplified? No it's not and with careful preparation this process will not only be simple, but second nature like breathing. To help facilitate this process we will be using *recipes*. Recipes are instructions on how to prepare successful relationships. Also included in the recipes are solutions to common mistakes we make when we are in relationships or seeking a relationship. By using the power of association coupled with everyone's appreciation of good eating, we will illuminate the truth about our nature and how best to address what we consider "problem behavior" in relationships. The difference between this book and other books is I don't suggest any absolutes or commandments (I'll leave those to GOD). I'm not an expert; I don't offer any tricks or magical solutions. I didn't write this book because I think I'm smarter than you, and therefore you need me. I won't sell some well phrased psychological b*s*. I'm not looking for an easy way to increase my market value in the dating stock exchange. I wrote this because what has helped me might help you. Plus, I need a way to get a free trip to Chicago to appear on Oprah, which brings me to the final difference. I like humor and will use it to lighten up the heavy load of our troubled minds. Like an operating room without the cutting and stuff. ☺

  Like with any good cookbook you "must" follow the recipes. These recipes will include ingredients, pots & pans, cutlery, utensils, definition of terms (slice, sauté, simmer, etc.), timers, spices, conventional oven vs. microwave, etc. The goal here is to "cook a good relationship." The steps that will help us cook a good relationship are the same steps that will help us cook a great meal. We start with fresh, wholesome ingredients, a clean cooking area, the proper cooking utensils, knowing how to cook, and knowing when the food is done. You will have to practice and develop your cooking skills on a regular basis. The development will take time and effort. There's no substitute for the work you need to do. Blind guessing is not a part of the process. If you are willing to depend on luck, by all means close this book now and use it for table decoration. If you would like something more reliable, then read on.

PreCooking

Pre-cooking starts with ungiving. Ungiving is not a new concept, just a new term. When talking to a friend about relationships he mentioned a female he knew who had trouble finding a good man. She asked him was there something wrong with her and if there was some obvious reason why she was still single, because her desire was to be in a relationship. He told her it might have to do with her unwillingness to ungive, and her unwillingness to make room in her life for what she wanted.

She owned two computers, both she received for free. She was pretty well off. Instead of giving the old computers away, that she didn't need, she was attempting to sell them and make a profit, even though she knew of friends who needed a computer who couldn't afford one. His question was, "Why should life give you what you need, when you're not willing to do the same for anybody else?" The other question inside that question was, "If your life is filled to the brim with yourself, how is anybody else supposed to fit?" Then he asked four last questions, "What do you want? What do you need? What do you deserve? Are they the same thing?"

Ungiving, simply put, is sacrifice or letting go. If you go to a car dealership and tell the salesman if he gives you a car you'll put gas in it, start it up, put oil in it, wash it, and make sure it runs, he'll laugh at you because these are mandatory tasks you need to do to maintain the car. What he wants to know is what you are willing to give up to get the car, how much you're willing to pay. You ungive fifteen thousand dollars and he'll give you the car. You let go of something and you'll get something in return. Too many times we want special treatment for proper behavior, to be rewarded for doing what we are supposed to. There are cases where young black men have been thrown parties for not going to jail, committing crimes, or taking drugs. No one should be getting a party because they didn't do wrong, they should get a party when they go out of their way to do more than right.

Special treatment is for special behavior. The same is true for relationships. Don't look for life to bend over backwards to give you your heart's desire when the only desires your heart cares about are its own. I use ungive because it's not giving to get, it's giving to become a better person, to deserve and make room for what you need and desire. The computer in the example had nothing to do with romance, but it had everything to do with her readiness and mindset.

Imagine packing a car full to the brim, trunk, back seat, and passenger seat, then inviting someone to ride with you. The problem isn't the spaciousness of the car; it's what you've packed in it. Initially everyone's life has room enough to fit others, however over years life becomes cluttered and space becomes scarce. This cluttering manifests in many different ways, the most prevalent is the "me, myself and I" syndrome. The idea that everything in life has to be related to, in some way centered around, about or concerning ME. Inside the me, myself & I syndrome, all pain has to be related to *my* pain and all joy is limited by *my* joy. If I can't conceive it, it doesn't exist. If I can't see it, it's not there. No principle can exist if it conflicts with *my* life. Most importantly, the only person I need is *myself*. But let's be honest, no one is the "end all, be all." The world does not rotate around nor gravitate toward any one person, including you. Ungiving the "I am the center of the universe" attitude will make room for the "let's share the universe attitude" that's needed to attract the life partners that reflect the special qualities we desire of them.

Being a good person is the foundation of good karma, but it is in no way the final destination. We want great rewards in life, so it is necessary to be great. We want abundantly, so we have to give abundantly. If you want to have plenty you have to make room for it.

Have you ever heard someone complain about their grades and blatantly say, "My teacher gave me an F but he's going to change it or I'm going to go off." I always want to ask if the teacher actually threw away their work and arbitrarily gave them an F or if they received straight F's and somehow expected a different grade for the course. The truth is they got what they deserved. What they wanted and what they earned were two very different outcomes. What are they for you? Have you done substandard work in relationship class and still expect passing grades? Are you deserving of the results of the high expectations that you have for your relationships? Most importantly, in all the getting and wanting and deserving, have you dealt with your

> **Secret Ingredients**
> Ungiving the "I am the center of the universe" attitude will make room for the "let's share the universe attitude" that's needed to attract the life partners that reflect the special qualities we desire of them.

needs?

What the complainers in the example above need are better studying habits, a tutor, or better listening skills. The grades will come with the acquisition of the necessary skill set. There seems to be a mixing up of what we have to earn with what we are owed. Learning to tell the difference between the two will have a profound effect on all aspects of our lives.

Everyone wants to be admired and revered and desires to have an extraordinary life, but this extraordinary life comes at a hefty price. The difference between greatness and mediocrity is consistency. Everyone has accomplished at least one major feat, but few have made the effort to make being amazing a habit. Make ungiving a habit. Continually make room for your dreams and earn the right to justly expect them to come true. If you are expecting or wanting a relationship, then you better make room for it. Cooking and preparing a relationship is a fulfilling task, but eating a fulfilling meal without room is a recipe for indigestion, gas and heart burn.

> *Secret Ingredients*
> **If you are expecting or wanting a relationship, then you better make room for it. Cooking and preparing a relationship is a fulfilling task, but eating a fulfilling meal without room is a recipe for indigestion, gas and heart burn.**

Preparation Before Cooking

Relationships are the exact same as meals. We decide what we want or don't want to eat. We decide whether we want to eat out or have it home cooked. We pay for it, and then we eat it. The preparation time and choice of food determines how good or bad our experience will be and whether or not we will do it again. This is basically how our personal lives work, although there is at least one major difference. With our meals we are aware of how we arrived at eating, whereas in our personal lives we don't know or recognize that we prepared the meal we're eating. We think it was prepared for us and we have no choice but to eat it. Consciously we are not aware of how we prepare our relationships.

When most of us think of relationships we think they are bigger than us. We think we can affect relationships but don't have any control over them. We think they just happen. The truth is we have absolute control of our relationships (we being the persons involved). Relationships "happen" just the way we make and allow them to happen. What we do not have control over is each other. Furthermore, we usually don't have an agreement about what relationships are and mean. We can look in the dictionary for a definition of a relationship or ask a psychologist to explain it to us, but in the end we all have our personal beliefs about what a relationship is and isn't; it's our own personal beliefs that we use to regulate our interactions. This lack of agreement as to what a relationship is leads to the problems and pitfalls we claim are the fault of relationships. If we changed how we approached relationships and established a common purpose and definition with the person we are involved with, then we would fully realize the control we have over them. Relationships are like good meals; you prepare them the way you want them.

Deciding. Budgeting. Shopping.

Making a good relationship is the same as making a good meal. Decide what you want to eat, set a budget, go shopping, make sure your kitchen is clean and then cook.

What kind of person do you want in your life? Don't be flaky with this first step. Don't just say I want someone nice, or loyal, or rich, or well built. Give a complete list of characteristics you want in a mate; everything from spiritual awareness to political affiliation. Be specific. If you wanted fish what kind would it be, catfish, perch, or salmon? Farm raised or wild? Canned or fresh? Be that detailed. Develop a real idea of the person you want. Know what they look and taste like. How are you going to shop for something if you don't know what it is or where to find it?

Believe it or not, you can get exactly what you want and ask for. The reason most of us settle for anything is because we haven't decided on something. The other reason is because we are not honest with ourselves. Most of us won't admit that the kind of person we want doesn't want us. Make your shopping list based on the truth and not fantasy. Don't be the person working at McDonalds, living with your parents, and catching the bus that refuses to go out with anyone who makes less than six figures and owns a car and a house. That's like wanting a dinosaur burger; you probably will die before you find one. Besides what you are really saying is, "If I met myself, I wouldn't date me." And if you wouldn't date you why should anyone else? Look at what makes you, you. Now honestly decide what kind of person you want in your life.

Don't get self-righteous or politically correct either. Some of us want snacks, superficial treats that are sweet and non-nutritious; something for right now until we make up our minds. Don't make your list for a relationship based on your sweet tooth. Make your list for a meal based on what will satisfy and keep you. If you want somebody for right now then get somebody for right now, but don't mix up the snack for the meal.

That stuff leads to cavities, stomach aches, indigestion and a great deal of other ailments we don't want.

Another important part of shopping is budgeting. You don't plan a million dollar banquet with a ten dollar bank account. When shopping for a companion, look for what you can afford. What I'm saying has nothing to do with money; it has everything to do with life style. Don't say you want a Godly, spiritual person when you're the biggest heathen on the planet, or that you want someone health conscious who works out everyday when you work out every leap year. Why would a saint make their bed with a sinner or a health nut get involved with someone who thinks being healthy is for nuts? In most of these cases we are shopping based on sight. We buy what looks good, not knowing if we will even like it. Then after we spend all our money splurging we end up eating ramen noodles for the next month. In relationships we call it the rebound or dating with no emotional ties. We've spent

---

Secret Ingredients

Some of us want snacks, superficial treats that are sweet and non-nutritious; something for right now until we make up our minds. Don't make your list for a relationship based on your sweet tooth. Make your list for a meal based on what will satisfy and keep you.

all of ourselves and now we're saving up for another meaningful relationship. Skip the madness. If you can't afford what you want, then save your money. In other words get your life together so when you look for that special person that special person will be looking for you. There isn't any shame in being broke. There's only shame in being ashamed of being broke. If you want a great deal in a mate you're going to have to have a great deal inside you and your life to afford them. Going shopping when you don't have enough money for what you want means you'll end up getting what you don't want. Spend wisely.

Once you've decided what you want and can afford as your main course, then you figure out what you want to go with it. If you chose steak then you'd probably pick a nice red wine and a vegetable. If you want a mate what do you want to go with them? Do you want to make a family, live from check to check, build a business, or travel the world? Do you want someone who is a sharp dresser or more casual? Do you want a rebel or a revolutionary? The reason you decide on this criteria before you go shopping is so you know in which section to look. Don't look for the secure, faithful mate in the promiscuous, financially irresponsible section. If you meet somebody during the work week while hanging out until the break of dawn chances are they are irresponsible, unemployed, or working a dead end job just like you. Don't look for fidelity in the "cheating on your spouse aisle." If you know the side dishes you want to go with the main course it makes it easier to prepare the meal. If you know what you want in and around a mate it makes it easier to know where to find them and to recognize them when you meet them. It will also keep you from getting with someone you don't want to be with. After you have made a thorough shopping list and set your budget then you go shopping.

    I don't know what kind of shopper you are so let's set some ground rules. Don't pick up the first thing you see at the first place you go. Compare price, place, and quality of product. If you're looking for a "God fearing" person don't pick the first person at the first church you go to. If you are a member of a church don't limit yourself to the members there. Visit other churches; spend time on the phone with different people; find out the nature of the church your visiting. Good people are like good groceries; they might be hard to find, but you can find them. Don't get desperate or rush the process. As Erykah Badu said, "I pick my friends like I pick my fruit." Keep your list handy. Shopping without a grocery list usually leads to impulse buying and a cart full of empty calories. Even if it means keeping the list in your pocket, do it. We make lists at times of clarity and honesty and sometimes have to be reminded of the decisions we've made during those times. If you have not trained yourself to control your impulses in small situations, you won't control them in big situations. Don't fool yourself, keep your list handy.

If you have the choice between two perspective mates make your decision based on how much they cost. What are you going to have to pay to build and maintain the relationship? Ask yourself if it's worth it. For me, long distance relationships used to cost me so much money and time it's ridiculous. It also cost me my ability to fulfill my intense desire for affection and interaction. When I wanted conversation and they didn't answer the phone, I talked to myself. When I wanted a hug I had to hug myself. When I wanted physical intimacy, well…you know☹☺! In the end I realized that I couldn't afford the distance. Relationships to me are close and immediate and what it cost me was more than I was willing to pay. Some commentators will say I'm shallow or superficial. I say, "You don't let me shop with your money, so don't ask me to live by your standards and opinions. If I can't afford it and you won't loan me the money to buy it I don't care about your opinion about what I buy." You can't live by what you don't believe and be a whole, satisfied, and fully functioning person.

Always check the expiration dates and compare it to your cooking schedule. If you don't plan on eating cereal until next week, don't buy milk that expires in a couple of days. Time is as important as content. Shopping based on time frames set by others is a breeding ground for bacteria and food poisoning. Eating food too old or not ripe enough, will both do you seriously wrong. Eating when you're not hungry will leave you bloated and uncomfortable. These are matters of time and timing. Getting involved before you're ready or after your interest is gone is no different. If you think over eating is nauseating, you will lose your mind, which most of us have done, by over dating and being over intimate. Time is not refundable so spend it like you can't get it back, because you can't.

Now that we've made our lists, set our budgets, and went shopping we have to prepare the meal. Let me backup for a moment. I didn't deal with shoplifting. If you've shoplifted, turn yourself in and hope for the best. Don't ask what shoplifting is, you know what it is. It's lying, faking the funk, perpetrating a fraud, being deceptive and dishonest to get what you can't afford. Though you think the food won't taste any different, it will. Karma is a cop with a long memory that might catch up to you ten years later. No matter the time frame it will find you and you will pay for what you stole. Put it back, put it back. I SAID PUT IT BACK!!!

Quit being hard headed and desperate. Stealing food and stealing souls are different and far apart. You are worth more than you give yourself credit for and can afford anything you give yourself a chance too.

Now that we've made our lists, set our budgets, and went shopping we have to prepare our kitchen so that we can prepare the meal. Put on your work clothes. We've got cleaning to do. When cooking, one of the most important tasks to do is clean the kitchen (you). Imagine being in a restaurant and the waiter brings out a delicious looking and smelling meal, but as the door opens you see a filthy roach infested kitchen with grease and grime all over the walls. It would kill all the appeal of the meal. At which point we would do whatever we had to do to keep from eating it.

The other reason for meticulous cleaning is we don't know what harmful bacteria and germs are in our kitchen. If someone gets sick there's no way to tell what exactly caused the illness. Then our only choice is to throw away everything including the food and start the whole cooking process all over. We don't want to do that, now do we? Our main goal is to prepare a healthy and great tasting meal, which is exactly what we're going to do! Now it's time to clean!

The kitchen we need to clean is you. In other words, you need to evaluate and reevaluate your opinions, discouraging aspects of your personality, and personal beliefs (or lack there of) surrounding relationships. When you are looking for spaces and places you need to clean it's important to be objective. Don't refuse to look in certain places because you don't think you need to. Our lives can have oil splatters and crumbs that we don't know about, so we must look thoroughly and clean the entire kitchen. For us to find some of these dirty spaces we actually need to get out of the way. Don't try to figure it out right now. It will become clearer as we move along. Step outside of the kitchen so you can see everything in the kitchen clearly. It's the same as looking for crumbs that have fallen, but you can't see them because you are standing directly over them. You have to step back to fully reveal the floor and then look down. The first step in this cleaning process is getting out of your own way.

Removing "You" From the Situation

One of the most valuable lessons I've learned is one of the most humbling, sobering, and insightful things I've had to come to accept. It's an important perspective that most of us either don't grasp or refuse to practice. Take a deep breath and brace yourself. Our lives will be more fulfilling and make more sense if we learn to remove ourselves from situations and honestly deal with what's really going on. Simply stated, remove the idea of "you" being the center of the world and the sole and solitary reason for every action that happens in it. We see the effects of not being able to remove ourselves all the time in general discussions where someone takes a statement personally and tries to argue you down by using themselves as an example. For instance, a woman says most men are dogs. An offended man replies how untrue the statement is because he's a good man, totally disregarding the operative words "most men" which are different from "all men" and are absolutely different from saying that he in specific is a dog. However, all he hears is a personal attack on his character and will argue to the death that the statement was made to belittle or insult him. Where if the man had responded based on "most men" he knew he might have been less likely to disagree so insistently or at least concede the point on a minor level. But thanks to "super me" defender and representative of everyone like me in the universe, that doesn't happen. We become bigger than truth, understanding, and better judgment and are therefore justified to inform the world of this fact.

    Our downfall comes when we ask the "what about me" question. To which I always reply, "What about you?" It may very well be that something happened for the benefit, well being, or punishment of someone else and you were just there to witness it and take notes for future reference - and that's it!!! But letting it go at that makes too much sense. We have to over analyze it.

When I was little a plane crashed at the same airport from the same airline I was supposed to fly out from the next morning to see my dad. I asked my mother what it meant. I told her I didn't want to die. I thought it might mean that I didn't need to go see my father or that I should take another airline. My mother assured me, that for me, it just meant the plane crashed and nothing more. I didn't believe her and tried to talk her out of making me get on the plane.

Now many years and four frequent flyer memberships later, I have to say, I believe her. But when it happened I was so caught up with me and how "I" was the one being affected that I refused to consider anything but that. One major factor I didn't consider was all the other passengers getting on the plane. As if my time to die meant it was everybody else's. Another factor was the condition of the plane that crashed. Just because one plane doesn't work doesn't mean they all don't work.

We can't see that when we blow ourselves up and put ourselves in the middle of every situation. All we can see is us and life trying to close in on us. Life happens because life happens, not because life is trying to happen to us. Look at what happens in life for what it is without you. Then you'll be able to understand what it is with you. Here's a news flash for you: life has caught up to everyone who ever existed and will catch up to you. You are not special, singled out, or doomed. You are just alive!

How to Clean Your Kitchen

If you are expecting a miracle cleaner you are going to be disappointed. If you are afraid of or despise hard work then you are really going to be disappointed. If you aren't willing to challenge yourself to live up to your true God given ability and get on your hands and knees and scrub, then you're probably going to throw this book out of the window. If you find yourself in a throwing fit then you are solely responsible if it hits somebody in the face. I accept no legal or moral responsibility for anything.

Cleaning your kitchen in relationships is the exact same as cleaning the kitchen you cook in. The dirtier it is the more time it takes. If you haven't cleaned since George Washington was president then you'll have to do some major scrubbing and use some powerful cleanser. It probably won't be easy. It's going to take time and sweat. You don't have a choice of brands and scents when it comes to the soap you'll use to scrub.

The only cleanser that can scrub the dirt out of your life is the *truth*. That's it, that's all, there is no more.

All the effort in the world won't help if truth isn't the soap you're working with. Trying to improve your life without truth is like cleaning without soap or water, a waste of time and energy. You'll only end up frustrated and convinced that there is no hope, but there is always hope. The only ones without hope are those who lie to themselves to justify living the way they live and suffering the way they're suffering. The truth is everything is possible. I don't mean figuratively either. I mean literally and immediately. If you're not willing to accept this fact, or at least try it out, your life will always be something other than what you want it to be. It's cleaning time.

Since our one and only cleanser is truth, we must honestly look at ourselves and what we do, regardless of whether or not we like what we see. Cleaning is using our cleanser to remove the dirt we find inside ourselves. The goal is to have a clean, whole, supportive life so we can prepare our relationships the way we need and want them to be. If you think your kitchen isn't dirty, clean it anyway. What have you got to lose except a little dirt? With that said, let's get to scrubbing.

First, clean the obvious dirt, the filth that you've been promising to clean for the last 100 years: grudges, trust issues, stereotypes about the opposite sex, disagreements from high school, overspending, playing mind games, anger issues, reservations about the opposite sex because of past relationships, selfish tendencies, the me syndrome, requiring others to live up to standards you don't live up to, thinking of yourself first all the time, being unwilling to compromise, being short tempered, being overly trusting without reason, giving without regard for your personal wellbeing, etc. These are problems that frequently are overlooked by you, but rarely go unrecognized by others and usually remain unresolved. This dirt is like any other dirt. No matter how great a chef you are or how great of a meal you prepare, a little of this dirt in your food will turn your treasure into trash. And I don't know anybody who enjoys eating food with hair in it.

These spills and stains in our lives are neither sanitary nor safe to overlook or walk over. I hear it now, the big question, "How do you clean those?" Most of us spend our whole lives trying to do it, but trying is not doing. The answer is simple, start cleaning and quit explaining why you can't. Talking about dirt is the most toxic kind of dirt that exists. We use it to justify not cleaning and to collect more dirt. If we did half of what we claim we need to do we wouldn't talk half as much about it. It might take plenty of scrubbing and scraping but it can be done.

Ask yourself, "Is holding on to all this dirt worth all the trouble it's causing in my life? Is it that I can't let go of these problems or that I don't want to let go of these problems?" If you said, "I can't let go," then let's look at the life-time smokers who say they can't quit smoking. When they're told by their doctors that one more cigarette will kill them, they all of sudden, out of nowhere, develop the ability to put the nicotine down. The truth is, they've always had the strength to do it, they just didn't see a reason to use it. As in cooking, we don't throw spices in if we don't think it will improve on taste and we won't clean if we don't think there's a reason to. But, once we find that reason, we are some spicing and cleaning fools. The question becomes, "How severe of a reason do you need?" Does your life have to fall apart, does it have to slightly unravel, or does it just have to need cleaning? When you find your reason you will clean, and it won't be as hard as you thought. As a matter of fact, you'll be a master cleaner and be motivated enough to start teaching others how to do it.

The way you get rid of dirt in your life is by becoming consciously aware of why you do what you do. When you become aware of the "why" behind your actions, you can become the "why" behind your actions and take control of your life. Let's say someone cheated on you and they gave certain "signs" that revealed what they were doing. But you didn't pay attention to the signs because you didn't think partner was capable of cheating. When you found out that they were unfaithful you broke up with them. You swore that would never happen to you again. Now, when you date, if you see these signs you are quick to address them or break it off. You think that you are in control, but you're not. Your fear of being hurt and cheated on is in control. And even if deep inside you know your partner is faithful you will still accuse them and bring negative energy into the relationship. Why? Because your fear is in control not you. That's why we act in ways we don't want to, for reasons we can't understand. That's why that dirt has been in our lives since forever and has the potential to stay until forever and a day.

Once we admit and understand the truth behind our actions we have the capacity to act freely. In the above example we see that we don't trust because we're afraid to be hurt. Once we understand and admit to that fear of being hurt we can choose to trust in spite of that fear of being hurt. If you don't know hurt is making your decisions you will never stop hurt from making your decisions.

Here's a simple example to bring the point home. In the previous example, do you think you are justified in being suspicious? If so, why? Think about it. If your answer was yes I'm justified because I've been hurt, cheated on, wronged, etc. you have proven my point. You are not reacting based on the fact that these signs are definite signs of cheating. Your reactions are actually based on the fact the signs are definitely signs that appeared when you were cheated on. Therefore in any given situation, whether or not there is justification outside of these signs, you are going to react the same way. Welcome to a life controlled by everything but you. Don't worry though; just like you let fear and pain run your life you can stop them. Pull out your cleanser and scrub that dirt out of your life.

Cleaning the kitchen is a process by which we examine our lives from then to now. Come clean with all the dirt that you have let control your life and decisions. Write them down when you recognize them. Have you become a womanizer because your heart got broken? Have you become a user of men after you were lied to and cheated on? Have you refused to need another human being because the ones you needed were never there for you? Write them all down. This is a list of places you need to clean. After you have completed your list reread it and address the issues one by one. Regain control of your life. Be empowered to make decisions based on what you want and need. If you want to need someone again, need them. If you want to love again, then love someone again. Let your fear and pain know that they don't control your life anymore.

You can do whatever you need to do and whatever you want to do!

How are we doing? Are you still there? Good let's get a little deeper.

We have to get in the crannies and corners, the not so obvious places, the crevices behind the refrigerator, the space under the stove, and the dust on top of the cabinets. Don't forget the crumbs in the corners, the grease stains that won't seem to go away, and the spills that have discolored parts of the floor. Scrubbing and cleaning these stains won't be easy or comfortable. You're going to need a whole lot of cleanser and muscle. These stains have bad attitudes and aren't going peacefully. These misguided notions are our parents', grandparents', and great grandparents' stains and lies. Our parents didn't know they were lies and didn't know they had passed them down to us. We have accepted them as truth. Although these thoughts may have served our parents, they need to be erased from our current belief system and conversation. They have been dug deep into our way of thinking so to get rid of them we must deconstruct and demystify them. These are the label-less forgotten items in the backs of our cupboards that have been ignored for years. Just because you have heard them your entire life doesn't mean they're true. It just means you have heard the b*s* for so long you have accepted it.

Relationship Myths

*Once a cheater always a cheater. . .*This statement is a gross generalization that allows us to condemn a person forever. We usually compare the cheater to the proverbial leopard that can never change its spots, implying that cheating is genetic. Well if that dumb idea is true then you should stop dating cheating leopards. Misogyny, distrust, commitment issues, and greed are learned behaviors. They are like lost money we found in the street, some dirty item somebody dropped that we pick up because it has some value to us. Behaviors like these can be changed and gotten rid of. Let's not mix up genetics with bad habits. One you're stuck with for life. One you're stuck with only if you stick with it.

Our disdain and contempt for cheating doesn't justify the irrational tendency to condemn someone who has once cheated, if in fact they have eradicated the negative behavior. A person who has cheated in the past, but has changed their ways should not be mistreated for past behavior. Everyone has the capability to improve themselves and their lives; don't get so caught up in your personal hang-ups that you can't acknowledge and act on this fact.

A person can change their behaviors.

All men are dogs, all women are gold diggers . . that's like saying all food tastes alike regardless of who cooked it. We know that's not true! Even though we are all cooked in the same world, we are made by different chefs. Therefore, our flavors and nutritional values are all different. If I gave two cooks vegetables from the same farm and a box of the same spices and told them to cook them, I guarantee the final products would taste different. We think every person and every situation tastes the same because we limit ourselves to the same corner stores and consistently buy the same personality type. Then, we continually run into the same type of person, time after time, and begin to think this dismal situation is our fate and there is nothing else available.

The only absolute is God. Sometimes we eat a dish with a taste so strong that it overpowers other flavors or makes them taste nasty. Think about eating something sweet after brushing your teeth. Not good, but it doesn't mean the food wasn't sweet. It means you need to wait until the aftertaste is gone before you put something sweet in your mouth. Simply said, don't get in another relationship until the aftertaste of your other relationships is gone because the aftertaste is ruining your ability to enjoy your food.

No two individuals are the exact same.

Love conquers all . . . Looking at the world around us kills this myth totally. Love is not a super hero who swoops in to save the day. Love motivates us to be super heroes so we can save ourselves. Love is the perfect spice, it motivates us to eat, it doesn't force us to. Don't fool yourself into thinking that putting love in a relationship is enough to get someone to participate in it. As mentioned before, love has many facets and purposes, but it's not the universal band aid or fix-all. Love gives us the opportunity to make the best of a situation and get the most out it, but it doesn't fix the state of affairs.

    Love is the fuel that gives us the strength and energy to conduct repairs. However, some situations are better left broke or at least left alone.

Love is a source of strength not invincibility.

I can change him, I can change her . . . No you can't. We change ourselves based on our experiences. Don't think you are so great of a happening that your mere presence will convince or force someone to change. It's God's job to deal with the inner-workings of a person's heart and motivations. Let Him do His job. If someone changes for you, when they are mad at you, tired of you, or not really happy with you the changes they've made are going to reflect it. We always hear "they were so different before" or "they've changed" and it's at this time we should know that it is not their behavior that is changing but their attitude toward us or our relationship. It's this attitude that is being reflected in their actions.

I'm not implying that we shouldn't desire others to change for the best. I'm saying we shouldn't try to force that change and that our desire for change should be because we want what's best for them, not what's best for us. Trying to change others for personal gain is capitalism and selfishness at its finest. Trying to inspire others to change for their personal health and well being is love. Ask yourself, "Am I in it for selfishness or love?" Make your decision accordingly. You are going to pay for what you buy.

Furthermore don't use relationships in an attempt to change your partner. Relationships can change somebody, but changing someone should not be the motivation. Look at this scenario. A man's dream is to run in a marathon and finish it. He becomes obsessed with fitness especially exercises that build his cardio endurance. For a year and a half he jogs everyday, eats healthy, and goes to the doctor regularly. The big day comes. He runs, he finishes, and that night he celebrates. The next day he sleeps late, eats junk and has no future plans to see a doctor unless it's an emergency. His motivation is gone. That's what happens when the relationship is the motivation. He/She works hard day after day to win your heart. Goes over and above any effort they would normally make. Then when they get you (run the race and finish it) they celebrate, stop making effort, and don't plan on doing that again unless it is an emergency. They have no more motivation. Where if the idea of being with you sparked an awareness of how they should change their lives to be happier and truer to themselves, after they got you they would still be doing what they did to get you because their motivation would still be there.

You cannot change someone.
They can change themselves.

My children and I are a package deal . . . Slow down. Speed kills. How do you tell your children not to talk to strangers, but then tell strangers they have to talk to your children? How do you tell a person that they have to accept you and somebody else, before they've accepted you? Besides, your children are too young to date. Date, get to know, and spend quality time with your perspective partner. Don't pressure them into liking kids or ask if they are willing to co-parent with you. Talk about family and listen to their responses. Mention the fun you have with your children and notice their facial as well as verbal reactions. Talk about their goals and dreams and see if they've made room for children. Don't forget that most of us will lie if we think it's in our best interest.

A slow pace is also helpful because familiarity and relationships change attitudes and beliefs. Think about your best friend. If two days after you met your soon-to-be best friend a major challenge to the relationship developed, the relationship would have been over. If after two years a major challenge developed there would have been a fight to maintain the relationship. The same concept applies. A good relationship can change someone's views about family and children. Bringing up extensive commitment before there is a relationship could end a potentially powerful relationship before it begins.

Last, don't let your partner and children spend time together until not letting them do so will affect both relationships negatively. Don't rush to push the two parties together. When they fit, piece them together. If they never fit then be man or woman enough to do what's in the best interest of all three parties (you, them, and the children) and end the relationship and remain friends.

You can't force someone into parenthood.

We have to be together at least six months before we have sex . . .There are only two categories that all sex falls under, marital and pre-marital. Either you will put out before marriage or you won't. If you are dedicated to no sex before marriage, let that be known when discussing core values and beliefs. Don't hold it back because you don't want to mention sex or are afraid of losing a "good catch."

A person who will leave you because of your choice to abstain from sex is not a good catch. Be firm with your convictions. Don't let your partner push the limits of your standards without being checked or they'll push until you or the relationship breaks. Either it's time for dinner or it isn't. If the food isn't ready let them find a snack. Letting them put their fingers in the pot will give them the impression that it's time to eat, or it will be soon!

On the other hand, if you will have premarital sex you are not obligated to let your partner know your criteria until they have met them. You don't lay out criteria for what someone has to do to get a kiss or what they have to do for you to love them. They do what they do, and if kisses and love come, they come. A person wants specifics about the when and how of sex because it is their main objective. Just because someone wants sex, it doesn't obligate you to give in or explain when you will or won't. If they ask what they did to deserve it simply say, "The right things." The reason is if your partner is only out for one thing they will do what they have to do to get it, even if it means waiting six months to a year, being in a relationship, or moving in. Then after getting what they came for they will do whatever they have to do to leave. If your criteria aren't known they won't know what to do and they will either give up or make it perfectly clear what they came for. Sex is like a "good job," people will lie and falsify resumes to get it!

Anthony C. Rucker

You are not obligated to justify when, where or how you'll have sex.

I'm independent . . . Independence means I don't need anybody for anything. As said in a great movie, "Why don't you wake up and smell what you're shoveling?"

Bill Gates, rich man that he is, still needs Charmin to make toilet paper and Ma Bell for phone service. Independence for him means having the ability to pay for it himself, which is all this new found independence everybody is claiming means: I now have money and means. It doesn't mean you don't need others, or that they are only good for one thing. Participate in a quick experiment to prove my point. Get a $100 dollar bill, then ask it to keep you company, to talk to you about your problems, to share a special moment with you, to plant your vegetables, to sew your clothes, and to fix your car. You get the point. It doesn't matter how much money you have, if there isn't another person involved it's totally useless. We need each other on so many levels. Even master card recognizes *there are some things money can't buy. . .*, and the sooner you get that fact straight, the sooner you can have healthy relationships.

Words are power and what you speak from your mouth will most likely manifest in your life. If you say the opposite sex is only good for one thing then chances are that's all you'll receive from them, which will leave you emotionally unbalanced with an emptiness you can't explain. So when you say, "They are only good for one thing," or "They can't do anything for me," take time to remember that's all you've expected and allowed them to be in your life.

Refusing help or courtesy doesn't make you independent; in most cases it makes you a hypocrite. If there was a contest where you could win free food for life everybody would play it like the lottery (another game where everyone wants something for nothing). Contest giveaways whether for movie tickets, money, or vacations are viewed as possibilities to get ahead, be blessed, or get lucky, but when a person offers the same services all of a sudden you're an independent super human who doesn't need or desire anything from anybody. Enough already! Put your misconceptions and bad attitudes back in the pretty boxes they came in, take them back to where you got them, and get a refund. Quit lying to yourself and everybody else. Besides, independence is something that is better seen than heard.

Refusing help or courtesy doesn't make you independent. In most cases it makes you a hypocrite.

Anthony C. Rucker

You should love me no matter what . . . Whomever I date must accept all of me, including my faults.

That sounds so good, but there's a catch. Your partner only has to deal with your faults if you're willing to deal with your faults. Faults are not necessary, nor are they immovable parts of our lives. To accept them as such is to admit defeat before the fight has begun. If you say, "I have a short temper and I'll have one forever. Deal with it if you love me," and your partner has good sense they'll tell you goodbye or to get a grip on yourself. If you say, "I have a quick temper but I'm working on it," then that's a sign you are looking to have a democratic relationship and not a dictatorship. Where there is no intelligent compromise there is no relationship.

Imagine going out to eat and the waiter says he only serves burnt chicken. You would tell him you're leaving. He says you're being unfair because that's all he has. In your mind you're thinking pay attention and you won't burn the food. The same goes for you, pay attention to your life and stop making excuses about burning your food. Accepting mediocrity and failure is very unappetizing. As much as we would like someone to live with our hang-ups like we do, it is not fair to ask such a thing. And how could someone honestly say they love you and want the best for you while they let you wallow in self-pity and contentment with mediocrity? That's not love, that's cowardice or complacency. Is insecure weakness what we want for ourselves, someone scared or inconsiderate? You can keep that. I want someone who is going to require me to work on me and to live up to my full potential.

Some of us will grow to despise someone who pushes us to succeed. We'll feel as if we are being pressured because someone is discontent with who we are. It's not about being unhappy with who we are. It is about loving who we are enough to want us to be who we can be. If you truly feel that way, like you're being pressured, you need to clean that dirt out of your life or ask your partner to clean the dirt out of theirs. Where there is contempt there will never be contentment.

A relationship is a privilege, not a right. No one has to be with you. You can't put unwanted demands on privileges. Where there's no agreement there's no relationship. We seem to think that a relationship is something life owes us. As if we have some divine right to another person's time and attention. Intimacy is a fruit that you have to work at growing. You don't have a right to just grab somebody's food and commence to eating. You have to till the earth, plant seeds, water them, de-weed the soil, and wait for it to grow and ripen. If you haven't done any of the work necessary to grow intimacy your only right to it exists in your delusional mind. You've got to earn it! Don't get mad when your flirtation or admiration isn't returned or think because your heartthrob didn't want you that they are shallow or superficial or ignorant. Understand that you need to get on your job because you don't get to harvest what you didn't plant.

When in a relationship your partner will love you, but that love isn't obligated to like nor accept whatever you do. Love is not blind, stupid, or gullible and it doesn't excuse you from responsibilities for your actions. You can't arbitrarily abuse and take advantage of somebody and then demand that your offenses be overlooked in the name of love. Love forgives and helps; it doesn't volunteer for target practice and play dead. If you want a puppet buy one. If you want a relationship act like it. If you make honest strides to change for the better love is supposed to be your advocate and plead your case for reconciliation. It doesn't guarantee forever, it fights for it. Remember that relationships are privileges and can be taken away. Let's not be disillusioned either, sometimes the best thing for a relationship is separation and love is strong enough to admit that.

Love doesn't mean that you will never be left, just that you will never be left alone. Support is not measured by distance it's measured by commitment. Understand this truth when you are being loved and when you love. Judge it on action not appearance. Most of what we see is what we make up in our minds.

Unconditional love is wonderful and if you can get it you are truly blessed. The problem is most of us don't want to reciprocate or be responsible to that love. The ones who cry about being accepted "no matter what" are usually the same ones who never accept anything "no matter what." We don't want the love to be active unless it's silent. "Accept me and shut up," that's what most of us ask of unconditional love. Take me and all my mess and don't say a word about it. That's a pimp-prostitute relationship not one of love. Who want's to be prostituted? How can you respect someone you prostitute? If we want unconditional love we have to accept the responsibility of being accountable and respectful to it. When we do we won't worry about how long love will be around or when it's going to leave. We'll be too busy enjoying love and wondering what beautiful, awe inspiring adventures it will be taking us on tomorrow.

Where there is no intelligent compromise there is no relationship.

Love me for my mind . . . My weight, build, body-type, or any combination thereof shouldn't affect a person's desire to be with me. They should love me for my mind and spirit.

Why? If I have a thing for freckles or breasts (big, small, or medium) or abs or feet or chipped teeth, should I give them up because you like me? Am I obligated to throw away my desires because you desire me? Of course not! You can't rob me of my freedom of choice. I have the right to date who I want when I want and that doesn't change because you've grown attracted to me. Humans are not possessions; you don't get them because you have enough money or resources. If you don't attract the subject of your desires it doesn't mean that something is wrong with you. All it means is that he or she is not attracted to you. Quit trying to get someone to like your cooking. Find someone who likes your cooking. Quit attempting to get someone to like you. Find someone who likes you.

Our spirits and minds are the most important parts of us, but they're not the only parts of us. We can't excuse our lack of appeal to someone based on our internal fortitude. We want more than spirituality and conversation in a relationship, so why should those be the only two factors used to make decisions about relationships? We want affection, compliments, sex, spark, arousal, and chemistry. How will we have these sensual components if we are coupled with someone who we don't appeal to or who isn't sexually attracted to us.

Too many times I've heard about the "superficial" person who wants the companion with the perfect body and looks. We talk about them as if they are wretched and wrong. The truth is we are attracted to that "superficial" person, but that person doesn't want us. If we didn't want them we wouldn't care about what they did and didn't like. Be honest, we are attracted to attractive people. We project our negative attitude towards an individual who wants an attractive mate. But what we are hiding is that we are unhappy about our physical selves. Furthermore, the object of our desire finds us unattractive, which reinforces our negative attitudes towards them and ourselves. Our anger is a reflection of our feelings of inadequacy and discomfort about how we look. If we weren't so concerned with our looks we wouldn't be so concerned with how others felt about looks. If we dealt with the personal issues we have with ourselves it would work out the issues we have with others.

Attractiveness is not based on how others feel about you or how many sexual partners you have. It's based on how you feel about yourself and whether or not you can sleep with yourself. The true source of appeal is security of self. My cousin used to mix together all colors and patterns, from plaids to stripes. I thought some of the stuff was quite awful and asked him how people reacted to his choice of dress. His reply was so insightful it changed the way I thought about appearance. He said they say things to him about his dress, but when he isn't affected by their comments and opinions and is obviously confident and happy with the way he looks they accept it, and even begin to think it's chic. After a while they would even ask him for fashion advice. I took this turn of events as a chance to carry out an experiment. I started dressing, what I considered crazy, mixing combinations that looked like I put them together in the dark.

When people made comments I addressed them with a smile and said, "I'm doing me." Just like my cousin my quirkiness became style and words went from criticisms to compliments. In the end we are all looking to feel better about ourselves. The path to self-acceptance comes from having confidence. When we have it whatever we do becomes attractive, hot, and appealing. It may not be what others are into but it will be labeled "style" instead of "silliness." The key element to this example is being secure with who and what you are. My cousin was totally secure and comfortable with what he was doing. Where there is no security or sense of self, there is no confidence. Where there is no confidence attractiveness becomes a game of chance. When we truly accept and appreciate ourselves we will draw others to us with that acceptance and appreciation of ourselves.

Warning, don't attempt to get people to like you so you can date them. Find people who like you, and date them. Why spend your time trying to convince someone to taste your flavor when there are those who love your flavor and would taste it without the sales pitch?

If you think sex shouldn't be a major deciding factor for a long term relationship you really should quit fooling yourself. Once you're in a committed long term relationship you are the only sex that person has access to for the rest of their lives, which makes it very important. Most of us have problems dealing with sexual frustration for minutes and days, how much more difficult will it be to deal with it for years and decades. Depending on the sex drive of those involved, sex could be the making or breaking point. Making a decision based on sex drive does not mean someone is shallow. It means they are honest. Imagine your favorite food. Imagine that you can't have it for a week, then a month, then a year, then a decade, then forever just because I don't want to eat it with you. A simple situation like that would piss you off and put you in a funk. I love french fries and ketchup and if I was told I could only eat them when someone else gave me permission I'd tell them where to put their permission.

Who are they to limit when I can and can't eat? I like sex a whole lot more than any food I've ever eaten and I'll be a different color and height before I curb my sexual craving for the rest of my life because somebody thinks I should. Not to say that we become sex slaves, but we are sex employees that have to work to keep our jobs. Don't work for a demanding boss if you can't keep up with the work load.

In addition to spirituality and conversation we want affection, compliments, sex, spark, arousal and chemistry.

Everybody deserves a second chance . . . No they don't. If I make you sick with my cooking and admit I don't know how, unless I take lessons or practice, there's no reason for you to ever eat my cooking again. Second chances are earned. An abundance of abusive relationships end in death because a second chance is given to someone who clearly has not made an attempt or resolution to change their behavior. Promises are made which are no different than me saying "I want to get better at cooking," but then I never go in the kitchen, read a cookbook, or take a lesson. How am I attempting to get better, the power of positive suggestion? You have a right and obligation to yourself to make sure that

I am truly getting better. If I am making strides and you don't believe them or recognize them you should keep your distance. Not because I don't deserve a second chance, but because where there's no trust there is no relationship. What kind of union will we have when you don't believe my words or in me, nor have I proven myself trustworthy. That's a formula for frustration and heartache, neither of which taste good.

The part where making this decision becomes tricky is when we hear words that reflect what we want to hear. The soothing sound and personal appeal draws us in like magnets. If we don't make an effort to resist we'll get pulled in and then they got us, back where we started. To stop this madness we have to fixate ourselves on actions. Actions can negate words, but words can't negate actions. If someone eats hamburgers but claims to be a vegetarian, is she or he a vegetarian? Not a chance. No matter how much they say they are. If I say I'm a meat eater but never eat any foods other than fruits, am I meat eater? No I'm not, not as long as the only things I eat are fruits and vegetables. Actions validate words. Actions earn second chances, words alone earn nothing.

Second chances are earned, not deserved.

Anthony C. Rucker

But he needs me, she needs me . . . This belief is a messiah complex. No they don't. If you fall over dead today they will be leaning on someone else tomorrow. No matter how precious or rare you think you are, no matter how much flavor you think you have, you are not the one and only. If you don't feed them they'll find another place to eat. If you were hungry and came to me for food and I refused you, would you give up on eating and accept being hungry? No! You would find something somewhere, just like the person who you keep trying to save and be there for, because they "need you," will find somebody else. They don't need you because they need you; they need you because you are convenient and reliable. There's no reason for them to need somebody else when you're doing such a great job as savior and messiah.

Being wanted by someone seems to excite parts of our make-up that we sometimes forget exists. We begin to think that this level of inner moving is only available to us through them. So we go out of our way to maintain their companionship, sacrificing everything short of our lives, but this feeling, this sense of wonder, is available to us with whomever we allow it to be. Being needed is wonderful. It gives us a sense of purpose and belonging, but don't let that allow you to be used and manipulated. A person who truly needs you will treat you with love and respect because they need you. A person who needs you for selfish gain will use and manipulate you and will always leave you feeling that way.

Being needed is wonderful. It gives us a sense of purpose & belonging, but don't let that allow you to be used and manipulated.

---

*You should act your age. . .*What exactly is an adult? There are two distinctive connotations that are heard on a regular basis. First the affirmation that someone is adult based on age, "I'm thirty years old. I'm an adult." Second the demand that someone's actions should be in line with their age, "You're thirty years old, why don't you act like it?" Which leads to two questions, at what age do you become an adult and where is the rule book that tells us how we should act at a particular age? It's obvious that most of us understand that there is a minimal level of knowledge and maturity needed to be considered an adult. What also is obvious is that most of us believe that turning a certain age automatically means we've reached those levels. The result is two sets of persons speaking about the same topic from different perspectives wondering why they can't come to some form of an agreement.

Anthony C. Rucker

The process of aging and becoming an adult is like going to high school. You are supposed to attend four years and then graduate. We are supposed to be children who eventually grow into adults. But just like someone can attend four years of high school and not graduate some of us have grown older and have not become adults. To graduate from school you need to put in a certain amount of work and satisfactorily pass classes that fulfill the requirements for a diploma. If you don't you either stay longer or drop out. Adolescence is the same; we are supposed to learn what we need to and become adults. Life, however, isn't so simple. We don't have principals and teachers to tell us if we've attained the minimum needed requirements of adulthood, there is no set standard for being an adult, there is no institution in place to regulate who graduates and who drops out, and just because someone has gotten older it doesn't mean they have graduated from adolescence.

When someone doesn't finish high school there next option is the GED, a chance to acquire the knowledge they were supposed to have already. For an adult we call it "growing up," the process of maturing into an adult so we can function and interact properly in the world. Problem, with no set standard and understanding of adulthood or being "grown," what are we really saying when we tell someone to "grow up?" Based on size and age it is obvious that a person has grown physically, so the component of growing that we want has to be that of mentality and maturity, but where do we go to get these aspects of our lives. We are supposed to get them from the adults who are responsible for us during childhood. If the adults in our lives lacked mentality and maturity, where are we supposed to get them from? The answer may be a school for soon-to-be adults; other cultures call it "rites of passage."

      Rites of passage is simply a system of mature and mentally capable adults who set up a mentoring program for children. The system is based on the needs and demands of adults in their society and the goal is to prepare them for their future. It is a structure that starts at home with parents and extends into the community. Everybody plays a part and has a responsibility in it. Therefore, if you have parents who haven't graduated adolescence they can get their GEDs from the Elders (teachers) and then pass on the knowledge to their children. Unlike school, if you fail no one holds you back but at least those dealing with you will understand that there is a level of maturity and understanding that hasn't been reached and understand that they are clearly dealing with a child and should therefore expect childish things. For those wondering why I put this in a book about relationships, it's because we are not born adults and a child's growing process will affect their adulthood and the quality of mates we have to choose from as adults. Being an adult is not guaranteed or inevitable. It is a planned process that requires as much focus and forethought as earning a diploma or a degree. We don't wake up one day as adults. We work to become adults and one day reach our goals. Adulthood is not a destination is it is a journey. Once we have made the journey, we will be more able, willing and skilled at maintaining healthy relationships. Put on your hiking boots and get to stepping!

There is a level of maturity, understanding & responsibility that comes with being an adult and it's more than just getting older.

These few examples of common misconceptions in our personal relationships are presented to give us a concept of what to look for and how to frame these stains and problems in a point of view that allows us to evaluate them outside of personal feelings and emotion. Once we've done this we can more honestly deal with cleaning them inside of our emotions. Identify the dirt in your life and clean what you can. Remember cleaning is using the truth to understand the "why" in what we do so we can become the "why" in what we do.

> **Remember cleaning is using the truth to understand the "why" in what we do so we can become the "why" in what we do.**

The Proper Cooking Utensils

As important as what we are cooking is what we cook with. You don't bake biscuits on paper plates or fry chicken in baking pans. We use the proper utensils for the particular task we're carrying out. Why we do this is simple, the utensils were made for the specific task at hand. Forks were made to pick up food. Spoons were made to hold liquids. Colanders were made to strain water from food. Frying pans were made for frying foods. Am I getting on your nerves yet? No? Ok! Baking pans were made for baking. Ladles were made for dishing out soup. Spatulas were made for flipping and turning. Can openers were made for opening cans. Blenders were made for blending. I'm being long winded for a purpose. We understand the concept of using utensils based on what they were made for. We don't try to drive chairs or take showers in cars. But when it comes to how we interact with each other we seem to lose our minds and throw this concept out of the window along with our common sense, better judgment, and intelligence.

Part of the issue is no one has ever taught us what part of ourselves we should use for the different situations we encounter, especially dating. We are supposed to do on the job training and figure it out as we go along. That sucks! School prepares us to function in society. College prepares us to work in society. Church teaches us how to love each other. Who teaches us to be in love? Who teaches us how to function in relationships? Who prepares us to work in a marriage and a family? Families are the foundation of every society. Supposedly growing up in a good family teaches you how to function in a family. Let's be honest, I've spent my entire life inside of buildings but that doesn't mean I know how to build one. I know what they look like and can recognize one when I see it. That's it! Just because you grow up in a family, it doesn't mean you know how to build one. You might know what one looks like, but what good is that going to do you if you can't build one? We have to learn how to build what we see. To build we need tools. Since we are cooking, I'll put it like this. I watched my grandmother bake pies and cakes for 18 years and can't make one like her to this day. We have to learn how to cook what we've seen and what utensils we need to help in the process.

There's a saying, "Good judgment comes from experience and experience comes from bad judgment." In other words the reason we are good at something is because we learned from being bad at it. That sucks too! There is one way of learning that I love the most, by example. Some say experience is the best teacher. I think for relationships that process is only for the hard headed and simple. I don't have to touch fire to believe it's hot. When I see the person who didn't believe yelling and screaming, clothes on fire and looking like a struck match, that's all I need. If we give up the belief that experience is the best teacher we will be more likely to teach our children in a proactive way. Most of us think we should let them find out like we did; like we enjoyed our experiences. We are responsible to teach our children how to use themselves emotionally, mentally, spiritually, and physically. Not so much by telling and instructing but by conversation, questions, and examples of our lives. Not in the vein of, "I'm so much wiser than you," but more in the vein of, "I am the same as you and maybe my life experiences can help you." We have to teach them what utensils they need to prepare healthy relationships. But how can we teach what we don't know or understand? First we need to learn it, and then we can teach others.

We need to get to know ourselves better in a more practical and functional way. We'll clear up some habits that aren't so good for us and come a step closer to the fun part, cooking!

Pots and Pans

Pots and pans are as universal as water. I don't think there is a question why we use pots and pans, but just in case there is I'll give a brief overview. The first reason we use them is to protect food from direct contact with the heat source, whether it be a flame or an electric eye. For those of us who use old methods of cooking beneath the earth's soil, pots and pans keep dirt off of the food. Besides protecting the food, they help to cook it evenly and in the manner we want it to. We use sauce pans to boil. We use skillets and frying pans to fry and sauté. I think the number one reason we use them is because they make it easier to deal with extremely hot food and keeps it from burning. When it comes to cooking I would say they are necessities.

In relationships the reason we use pots and pans is the same. Follow me on this one and use some imagination. Life is a red hot heat source used to cook us and we need pots and pans to be able to prepare relationships and experiences without burning them and ourselves. Living is our experiences with any and everything. It is our comings and goings from birth until now. It is every experience we've had with everybody we've ever met. These experiences have the ability to burn unforgettable images and ideas in our minds and affect the way we live the rest of our lives. They have the ability to burn some memories beyond recognition and palatability as well. It can also prepare the experiences in a million different ways based on our knowledge of cooking. Life is a multi-purpose stove and oven that can handle all of our cooking needs. It sounds corny but work with me. The only limits on cooking are our imaginations and the utensils we have to use.

    The pots and pans we use to protect ourselves from the heat of life are our emotions and intellect. Everything in our lives is filtered through, cooked on, our emotions and intellect. They keep our experiences from being consumed by the heat and help us to prepare experiences that we can digest and process. Particular emotions and modes of reason help us to prepare our experiences in different ways. During highly emotional times we cook our meals in the wrong pan, at the wrong temperature, and wonder why the food tastes nasty. It tastes nasty because we don't know what we're doing. We're really bad cooks, preparing really bad food and are quite pissed off about it. We have eaten so much trash we could double as garbage dumps. We have misused our emotions and intellect to the point that some of us have damaged them beyond use. We are at a point where if we don't repair them we will be cooking toxic meals for the rest of our lives. Our emotions are so scratched and chipped that they have become just motions. Our intellect has gone from guaranteed non-stick to I-bet-you-every-thing-sticks-every-time. Rarely if ever, do we use both intellect and emotion in conjunction with each other to make the meal of our dreams.

I hear them again, those big questions. "How is he going to tell me I don't know how to use my emotions and intellect? Who does he think he is? Is he telling me there is a proper way to use what's inside me?" My responses are, I'll tell you like this, most times we don't know what we're doing, I think I'm me (last time I checked), and yes there is a proper way to use them. If you or your psychiatrist, psychologist, or life coach doesn't agree, I'm cool with that. All I'm asking is, if there's not a proper way to use them, why are you going to a psychiatrist, psychologist, or life coach? Help me out. Deep inside we know there should be order. We know that life isn't supposed to be some randomly happening event that uses us for fun and games. However, we have an innate ability to mix up and confuse situations and make them hard to figure out. To hide the fact we are feeling helpless when it comes to making sense of what's going on, we conclude that there must not be a way to make sense of it all and therefore we're normal. Since we're normal there's nothing to figure out, this is just how things are. Not so. Not so. Not so. Why give up so easy? I know life hits like Mike Tyson but don't wimp out. Keep fighting. There's hope. Enough of the small talk, let's get down to business.

Webster's defines emotion as a mental state that arises spontaneously rather than through conscious effort and is often accompanied by physiological changes; a feeling: *the emotions of joy, sorrow, reverence, hate, and love.* What I add to Webster's definition is that we can train ourselves so that our spontaneity is in balance with what is going on in our lives. We can train ourselves and instincts in the same manner we do when we cook a meal over and over again. After awhile we do not need measuring cups or directions, we remember what to do and how much of each ingredient to put in. We can "eyeball" it. I also add that we are already trained, but don't understand how and don't have a conscious knowledge when we are using that training.

For example take the words, "I don't want to kiss you." If they come from someone who we really want to kiss they would bother us, lead us to question ourselves, and would most likely hurt us. If they come from someone we are not attracted to and don't want to kiss they would be refreshing, relieving, and most likely make us laugh. Why, because we have prior concepts of what is and isn't desirable and pleasing to us. If someone we never met and know nothing of dies we don't cry, wear black, or go to the funeral. Why, because we have no association or relationship to them. In these cases our intellect and ability to reason have already decided what pots and pans (emotions) to pull out or maybe to pull out none at all.

The only differences in those examples are the factors that we use to measure the value of the situations. Our reason is an automatic pot selector. Being led by reason sounds robotic but it is the way we work. We try to deny it. Our emotions are not purely based on feeling. They are based on feeling and reason, and for good reason. If we didn't use reason to keep our feelings in check we would all be flighty, indecisive, emotional wrecks that were as flaky as a Betty Crocker pie crust.

We get into deep water when we don't realize that we've been incorrectly taught that we are slaves to our emotions and are not supposed to regulate them. The issue we have with regulating our emotions is coming to grips with the idea that you can be intellectual and spontaneously feeling at the same time. Since we don't know how to be intellectual and spontaneously feeling we assume that we aren't supposed to, but we are. Could you imagine being in a kitchen where the pots and pans tell us which one we should cook with and we follow their directions? Of course not. Emotions are the same in this regard; they are supposed to be used by us and not us by them. Not to say you can control what emotions you initially feel, but that you can decide what emotions to use to properly prepare a situation so that it can be healthy and helpful to your life. Feeling is the initial reaction our emotions have to a given situation. Using our emotions is when we assess a situation and use the emotions best suited for the occasion.

Once I was in a long distance relationship. After a couple of months I came to the conclusion that I was not satisfied with the relationship because of our limited access to each other. I called her and told her that I was ending the relationship because I was lonely and longing for intimacy. I decided that before I cheated or lied to her about my feelings or actions, I would part as a friend. She wasn't sure what to feel. After contemplation she concluded that she could be sad, but decided to be happy. She was happy that I cared for her enough to be honest with her and to show respect for our commitment. Instead of automatically being sad she looked at the situation and carefully considered it. She realized that even though there was a desire to be sad, she found a reason to be happy because of the respect that I showed her and the friendship we developed.

Anthony C. Rucker

We can select the pots and pans we prepare our lives in. It is the meanings we assign to the events in our lives that evoke the emotions we process them with, not the events themselves. If we love flowers and associate happy thoughts and pleasant memories with them and one day they all die, the value we've placed on them would result in us associating their deaths with sad thoughts and unpleasant memories. But the death of flowers in and of its self is a stage in the circle of life where things grow, die, fertilize and feed new life. No matter how much value we assign to the flowers their fading away will never be more than that.

When we assign meaning we assign emotions. When we decide what kind of food an experience is, we decide what pot to cook it in. We pre-select the emotions we experience by developing an understanding of what experiences mean. When we understand death, we associate it with sadness and loss. When we understand winning, we associate it with happiness and joy. The basis of our emotional make-up and interaction with each other is based on our values, beliefs, understandings, and intellect. When we understand how we choose our emotions we can choose them wisely. By now I know everybody's calling me crazy and a quack but let's do some role play to clarify.

A child is crying because she has lost her favorite toy. Most of us would feel some sort of regret about it. If we know before hand or find out later that the child's parents are billionaires, most of our regret would turn to indifference because we have associated wealth with the ability to fix or replace whatever's wrong. We then would probably express disgust at a "spoiled rich-kid" crying for nothing. Every emotion we are feeling has been pre-programmed for the situation based on our beliefs and reason, none of which deal with the fact that the child may have developed a concept of her toy that is just as strong as our beliefs and concepts about wealth. For a child with no understanding of money and what wealth means, a toy could be the beginning and ending of her world. When the toy is gone so is her world and she reacts that way. So while we are seeing a spoiled child the child is seeing a heartless adult. Both emotions are valid based on what each of us has lived, but neither is a productive or healthy way to process the experience. By thinking the child is spoiled we look at her with disgust. By thinking we're heartless the child develops contempt for adults. Now we have a world created by emotions that is not true to the situation.

We make prejudicial assumptions based on how we feel even when what we feel has nothing to do with the situation, a case of the pots telling the cooks which one to use. To avoid this trap we have to learn to look at life experiences in the context of what they really are.

The words "I hate you" don't hurt. It is the concept and beliefs we assign to them that hurt.

How we can apply this concept in relationships is by understanding that the feelings we experience are more a result of what we believe than what really happens. Therefore, we have to use our intellect to figure out if the feelings we are using in a given situation are the right pots for the meal we're preparing. For instance if your fiancé does something that hurts you it doesn't mean that you operate from that hurt and become sarcastic and vindictive until you're over it; even if you feel that's what you should do. The reason is, the longer you're sarcastic and challenging, the longer the contempt will grow and the longer it will take to recuperate from it. What your intellect should come in and say is that the act could be cooked in the anger & disappointment pot, but if we want to create a healthy relationship we should cook it with honesty, reconciliation, and forgiveness in the hope pan.

The feelings we experience are more a result of what we believe than what really happens.

---

*Relationship*Cookbook

Relationships are like meals; we cook them until we get a taste appeasing to our palette. If we cook a meal in anger and disappointment pan we're not going to like it. The more we cook in that pan the more we will hate the relationship. The reason we continually revisit someone's real or supposed wrong doings and mess ups, even after they have been resolved, is because they have never truly been resolved. We attempted to process a resolution with scratched up dirty pots that have left a negative residue on the resolution, which has left a bad taste in our mouths. Even still, our minds tell us we're justified and since we're justified the fault for the relationship still tasting nasty is theirs. Here we are using intellect to justify our feelings, which is what we always do. We always seek to justify the way we feel based on some tangible fact or event. No one justifies emotions based on feelings. That's like saying, "I'm angry because I'm mad." You're angry because of specific events or happenings that have upset you, not because you're mad. We are unconsciously trained. We must make that training conscious.

The question becomes, "This is how and what I feel, but is this how I should act or what I should do?" As stated before it's our nature to justify feelings with facts. What we feel only exists to us inside of the meaning we assign to events in our lives. What exists between people is what happened and what will be done to address that happening. When we justify acts with feelings we take a world that exists and try to fix it based on a world that doesn't. That even sounds crazy, which is what we're called when we become overly emotional. We don't recognize that we consider an overload of emotion crazy. If you think I'm just making stuff up think about someone who has no control over their emotions, what do we call them? Crazy, that's what we call them. So in are minds when we become justified and led by our emotions we, in our own words, are acting crazy. With that in mind, let's be honest with ourselves and find the balance between emotion and intellect that will keep our pots and pans clean.

Let's be honest with ourselves and find the balance between emotion & intellect that will keep our pots & pans clean.

Another part of using pots and pans is maintenance. We have to clean, repair, and, store our emotions properly or they will become useless to us. For some strange reason, we think we can take chipped, beat-up, trampled, dirty, worn-out, emotions and make new fresh meals from them. We are soooooo smart.☹ Maintaining emotions is not a complex act. Think about how we take care of our pots. When we cook we make sure we use one made for the specific task. We watch them to make sure we don't burn them or the food. We clean them out after we use them, then put them in the cabinet and store them until we use them again. We must start emotional maintenance by using the emotions specified for the tasks or situations at hand. Don't forget the difference between using and being used by your emotions and feelings. Process the situation and use the appropriate emotion. Don't use all your emotions in every situation. Embrace what you initially feel, but you are not obligated to act on what you initially feel. We don't use joy to process abuse or shame to process success. We use emotions that help us to process, come to closure with, and move on with our lives.

When we are using our emotions don't leave them unattended. When we leave our emotions to monitor themselves they end up burnt, along with whatever we are cooking in them. Don't be fooled into thinking emotions will maintain themselves. Being happy doesn't maintain happiness. We stay happy when we do things to make ourselves happy. Happy doesn't come over to the house, pick us up, and take us out for a night on the town. Even anger doesn't maintain itself. Every one of us has been angry for so long we have forgotten what we were angry about. All we remembered was that we were mad and were staying that way. Every emotion has to be watched and maintained. When that emotion has run its course or is no longer useful we have to switch to the appropriate one.

Sometimes we think because we are in love and in a loving relationship we should only need our pleasant emotions. Our tendency to categorize events in our lives is usually the source of this kind of thinking. We forget that we are in a relationship with a human being and we will need every emotion available to human beings. We are multidimensional and use a wide range of emotions all the time every day.

After we use our emotions we should check them for damage and dirt because what ever is left on them will end up in the next meal we use them for. Don't we always ask how the same circumstances keep happening to us? Don't we always ask why certain situations always bring out a part of us that we would rather not deal with? Don't we always ask why we act in ways we don't understand? This is because there are remnants of past experiences hanging on to our emotions that we need to clean off. Walking away from a situation and starting over clean is a myth. We will walk away clean only if we clean before we walk away. When we are not good with intimacy chances are it's because the last time we used it, it got all scratched up with betrayal and we haven't repaired it. When we avoid love chances are it's because the last time we used it pain got stuck on it and we haven't cleaned it off. So every time these situations present themselves we start having adverse reactions and falling into old habits. Most of us think it's because we need more time to get over a bad experience, but it has nothing to do with time. Twenty years later we will be doing the same things. All that happens over time is that we forget the source of our adverse reactions and end up having to go back to them again to deal with what we were trying to avoid in the present.

There seems to be an assumption that emotions are pure and unable to be defiled like art. Emotions however are far different than art. Art is something we do and bring into being. Emotions are a part of us and are what we live. Therefore everything that we experience influences and becomes a part of our emotional make-up; that emotional residue and clutter can cause our emotions to be defiled. Unless we consciously address the affects of our experiences they will attach themselves to our emotions any way they can and adversely affect the way we use them.

We clean emotions by acknowledging that they are good and necessary and not the source of what we've gone through or experienced. They are simply what we felt. We have the gift of free will and must acknowledge the part it plays in our lives. We use free will to determine how we use emotion. What we emote is not wrong, how we react to those emotions can have negative consequences. When something "goes wrong" it is not because we used emotion. It is because we exercised our free will and what happened is a result of that choice. Once we vindicate our emotions and validate that they are good and necessary we clean them, making them usable again. When we remove all the negative stigmas and stereotypes we associate with emotions we are subsequently removing adverse reactions and reoccurring unwanted behaviors that we attribute to our emotions. We are freeing ourselves to use them to our benefit, instead of being used by them to our detriment. Cleansing our emotions is a deliberate act that has to be purposely carried out. It's not something that will just happen over time.

Clean pots aren't stored on the counter or stovetop. What would happen if we kept all our pots and pans there? What if when we cooked and cleaned we didn't move them either? What would they look like after a month? They would all have small speckles of

---

Secret Ingredients
Cleansing our emotions is a deliberate act that has to be purposely carried out. It's not something that will just happen over time.

grease, food and dust on them. We would be tired of them and would look at them with disgust. To keep those pots and pans clean we would have to wash most of them almost everyday, and there would never be room to cook without having to move a million things around. That's how we look when we bring every emotion into every situation. We look and act sporadic and confused because we are cluttered with emotions that have nothing to do with the situation.

    Let's say there is a person in your life that is habitually mean and nasty to everyone they interact with. I mean nasty to the point most people only deal with them when they absolutely have to. But every time there is an altercation between you and them, you begin questioning yourself and your self-worth because of how they treat you. You also question your love for them because you think that if you truly loved them and let it show they wouldn't treat you the way they do. What you've done is brought out extra pots that have nothing to do with what's going on. Let's use our intellect and select the pots we need for the situation. There exists a person who treats everyone equally bad regardless of how others love and treat them. They are habitually spiteful and mean except when they need something and they show no knowledge of or remorse for their actions even when they hurt someone. Is this a situation where love and self-worth are the best pots to use? Hell no! The only way you can say yes is if you think you are so far away and different from everyone else that you have the ability to affect change whenever you so desire and that by not affecting change you have failed the nasty person because you didn't use the full range of your super powers to change their lives. If that's true, you super hero you, then you need to trade in your cape and get a new profession.

Why would you judge your worth and ability to love based on someone who spits on it every chance they get?

Why would you judge your worth and ability to love based on someone who spits on it every chance they get? You make those self-worth judgments based on those who show an appreciation for them. We bring in extra opinions, ideas and emotions just because we can and our only justification is because we wanted to. I want to fly without an airplane, that doesn't mean I should try to do it. Put away what you're not using and protect your emotions from situations where only bad things are likely to happen to them.

Being sporadic and dishonest with the use of our emotions has led us to revile the part of us that makes our interactions with each other more than just actions.

Refusing to use our emotions and intellect in a system of checks and balances has left us off balance and habitually falling over even the simplest situations and problems. Once we regain our balance it will enable us to cook a great meal. When we learn how to use what God gave us, instead of letting it use us, we will live more emotionally and spiritually satisfying lives.

Conventional Ovens vs. Microwaves

As important as what we cook is what we use to cook it. Now a day, we have microwaves that prepare food ten times faster than the stove and oven. With this new technology has come the fear of radiation, the damage it does to some foods, and the effects it will have on us in the future. It saves us time though and for now we are willing to run the risk for the convenience. For most of us the oven wasn't a "bad" invention and served its purpose quite well, although it took up a great deal of room, was fairly expensive, and was hard to move when it broke. On account of its resilience and dependability we have continued to stick with them. The correlation to our lives is an exact mirror image. In relationships these ovens are our values and beliefs. Like ovens, our values and beliefs have changed. Some have been streamlined and modified based on new technologies. Some, like the old oven, have remained the same, hard to move. Each one of us has our personal preferences and how we cook is a matter of personal choice. Mastering the use of our beliefs and values and understanding how those beliefs and values contribute to the development of our relationships will better enable us to prepare our relationships.

A strange quality about values is that most of them are shaped and set by the age of six. That's right, sixty to eighty percent of what we believe is locked in place before we get out of the first grade. Of course there are additions and deletions, but for the most part they are the same; which means that right now at the ages of eighteen, twenty-one, thirty-five and fifty-six we are still acting on what we learned at age six. Chances are that what we remember about how we came to accept what we believe is kind of fuzzy and faint but that doesn't stop us from using it to measure and make sense of how we live today. This tendency leads to some serious issues, like most marriages ending in divorce, domestic violence, misconceptions about each other, etc. We need to become overly familiar with the basis of our values and ask whether they still apply.

There are moral standards like honesty, compassion, love, and respect that are going to be viable and relevant as long as we exist, whereas there are beliefs based on social and cultural concepts that might not be relevant today. There was a time if a woman wasn't married by thirteen or fourteen she was an old maid. There was a time when hard physical work was a symbol of strength and manhood. There was a time where "shacking up" was a sign of moral depravity and a lack of good home training. Today, if a girl gets married at fourteen somebody is catching a statutory rape case, if you work hard you need more education so you can get a better job, and if you don't live with someone before you get married you're taking un-needed risks.

I'm not taking a stance for or against any particular value right now. What I'm doing is looking at our beliefs in the context of the times we live in and asking if they still serve us the way they did when we were six and will they sustain us in our present relationships. I'm also asking if we know the origin of our beliefs and if we don't, once we do, will we still accept them.

Superstitions are a result of accepting beliefs without understanding them. Black cats being bad luck comes from a legend about a queen who was a witch that turned herself into a black cat and walked across a person's path right before she killed them. Walking under a ladder is supposed to be bad luck because when it leans against a wall it forms a triangle. Since triangles are symbols of the trinity, walking through a triangle is supposed to represent a contempt or breaking of the trinity. Knocking on wood comes from the belief that spirits live in trees. The Druids would knock on wood to get the attention of the spirits within the trees so the spirits would acknowledge their requests. How many of us believe any of that? How many of us knock on wood and avoid walking under ladders?

Now that we know the origins of these superstitions some of us are thinking about how dumb they sound and how foolish we've been to practice them without knowing where they came from. Our values are close and meaningful to us, but some may be as foolish as these superstitions. We'll never know unless we revisit them and find out if they've outlived their usefulness. One other possibility we need to consider is that the beliefs instilled in us contain the personal opinions of the person(s) who passed them on to us. In some of the beliefs women have about men I hear the fear and opinions of their mothers and the same with sons and fathers. We're passing down personal grievances dressed like facts of life and the children suffer for them. They end up paying for the transgressions of their parents. That's not fair in the least.

There are a few values I want to address specifically, the rest I leave up to you. Again, I'm not the "answer man" and what I say is not law. These are my insights and beliefs and you should only accept them based on your choice not my suggestion. I may seem wise or knowledgeable, but I am still fallible and should be challenged and held accountable for what I say and present to you. With that said we'll move on.

We live in what I call the "Mc World," a place where we want everything now and expect to get it now. We move like time is running out, therefore anything that saves time is cool. If there are risks or repercussions, it's okay as long as the risks are minimal or not known. We figure as long as something doesn't overtly harm us in the here and now we will worry about the future when we get to it.

Instant gratification has become the standard on which we base our lives. Saving time is the biggest business on the planet. There are time saving methods on working out, on eating healthy, on traveling, on shopping, on preparing meals, on meeting others, even on developing relationships. There are three million ways to save time doing everything. In some cases I think it's wonderful. The invention of the train and boat I like. To be able to cut travel time and make the world smaller and more accessible opens up so many possibilities. At the same time, neither cause harm nor adversely affect the earth. In some cases, I think saving time is the worst thing that has happened to us. For example, the gun was an invention designed for saving time. Although a tool for protection and hunting food, it has served as a tool to aid man in furthering the reach and level of destruction, war, vengeance and anger. The more we "save time" the more we depend on automation and technology and the more impersonal and desensitized to human beings we become. The result is a degradation of human interaction to the point where we view other human beings as time savers or time wasters. We measure others by how they function in our schedule. *I don't have time, life is too short, we're not getting any younger, time is money,* how many of these sayings do we use on a regular basis? We are hoarding time like it's not only the most important aspect of life, but like it's the only aspect of life.

When I worked as a waiter I was on the night shift. Sometimes the place would be packed and sometimes it was totally empty. One day it was just me and one other waitress working the entire night and she was pregnant and not feeling well. She asked if I would mind if she went to her car and took a nap since we didn't have any customers. I said no problem only to find out fifteen minutes later there was a big problem. We went from totally empty to almost completely full. I couldn't go get her because I was seating patrons and taking orders. She was out cold. I ran around like a lunatic and messed up every order I took. Customers got pissed, called me words my mama wouldn't approve of and made some gestures that I think were meant to hurt my feelings. When she finally got back I thanked God, Moses, Jesus, and the twelve disciples. She giggled when I told her how I messed up everything. She said, "Baby, I forgot to tell you a rule of waiting tables. It's better to give great service slow than to give bad service fast." I say the same to you.

In our hurry to maximize our time on this earth we tend to give each other bad service. We rush from here to nowhere. I can't count how many times I've been cut off while driving, or how many drivers have almost caused accidents running red lights. I always ask myself, "What destination is worth risking life to get to?" When dating I here women talking about their biological clock. My question to them is, "Is having children worth risking having them with a man who won't fulfill his duties as a man and a husband?" What are we willing to sacrifice in the name of time?

As said before microwaves save time but are not suited for all occasions or are safe under all conditions. If you don't believe me put metal in your microwave and see what happens. Don't do it. It will cause a fire and maybe worst. There are some experiences that are not safe to rush and relationships are one of them. Trying to streamline relationships puts us into very painful and adverse situations that usually lead to us fearing and hating relationships and our partners. Even when couples are put together based on compatibility studies it still doesn't account for personality and life experiences and takes away from the possibilities of the "unlikely couples" that come together and make great marriages. I think the other factors that get over looked are that interacting with others makes us better at it and when we maximize time we minimize friendships. Formidably, we are not just minimizing friendships; we are diminishing human interaction to the extent that we eliminate the possibility of developing relationships.

Moving too fast also builds up expectations that for the most part are anticlimactic. We put faith in variables and factors instead of each other, expecting these variables and factors to solve our problems. What we don't recognize is that our problems are a result of our inability to functionally interact with each other and that minimizing that interaction will not make us better at it. Minimizing interaction will make us worse. Think about calculators. They were made to simplify the math process and to make math more accessible. Now some classes require a calculator to take them. The result is we have straight "A" students who can't do math without a calculator. They haven't become better at math, just better at using calculators to do math. If our efforts to conserve time dismantle our ability to be proficient at creating relationships, our efforts are being counter-productive. It will eventually render us so inefficient at relationships that we will have to learn how to interact on basic levels all over again.

What we do with time is one of the main villains we fight against. We use it as a weapon of defense to limit our interactions. I have heard women say, "If he isn't ready to get married in a year then we're breaking up." But what if he was ready to wed in one year and a month? Is a month worth throwing away the possibility of forever? We consider time a form of currency and expect a profit in return for spending it. This desire for a tangible return forms a mind set where we look for guaranteed returns on time. When dealing with humans the only guarantee is there is no guarantee. Now we find ourselves in a position where we expect what we can't get. Therefore we look for ways to get guarantees or as close as we can come to them. We join singles groups, call chat lines, use dating services, take compatibility tests, speed date, and read books about relationships (in this case it's alright because I don't offer guarantees). We don't want to waste our time. The crazy part is until we die the only thing we're guaranteed to have is time. I know we want to get to the "good part" as quick as possible but getting to the "good part" before we're prepared to receive it isn't good and sometimes the person who you weren't willing to make the time for will make the best life partner for you later in your life.

My wife and I had a respect for each other when we first met, but didn't like each other at all. We shared intellectual and artistic conversation and that was it. We both thought the other had major issues they needed to work through. For four years we were friends and dated everyone except each other. It wasn't even an option. Four years later we got closer after a near family tragedy. Our interaction revealed changes in attitudes and maturity that both of us had made. We were both vegetarians with an intense desire for family and spirituality. Fasting was now a regular practice for us and so was a love for working with children and uplifting our people. Add prayer and some passionately honest conversation and now we're married.

Dating without becoming friends is a microwave concept. It allows two individuals to go from strangers to a couple without ever knowing each other. Then they go from dating without knowing each other, to married without knowing each other, to separating without knowing each other, to divorced and hating each other. The time they spend together is used strictly for romance and entertainment. There is no preference to actually be friends because friendship is not a considerable option.

It was the institution of friendship along with the appreciation of others, even when they weren't the obvious or ideal companion that opened the door of opportunity on the wonderful life I live now. I made the decision that I would get married when I was ready and only to a woman who was all of what I wanted. Not part, half, or three quarters, and I refused to consider time in the equation. I had chances to marry other women before her who were close to what I wanted, but refused. The final result was I got what I desired and deserved and so much more.

The last ideal I want to address about friendship and dating is the belief that we shouldn't date friends because it will mess up our relationships. I don't know where this idea came from, but I can tell you where I want it to go. What ends friendships is not unsuccessful dating; it is caused by irresponsibility and valuing lust over friendship and loyalty. The biggest pile of manure I've ever heard was, "I love/like you too much to be just friends." All these words mean is, "I can't or refuse to take responsibility for my feelings and actions and if you won't cater to my desires I can't be around you." Love doesn't throw anyone away when love isn't reciprocated. When we get rid of a relationship or a person because we like it "too much" it's because we lack control.

People who want to lose weight don't avoid sugar because they "like it too much." They avoid it because they don't have control over their desires and they will over indulge to the point of self-harm. We can't blame the sweetness for our lack of will as we can't blame love for it either. Besides, friendship is not the booby-prize or the second place trophy. When we look at friendship like it is second best we reveal a confession of what we truly think about friends; they're only cool when there's no romantic interest. This means that those we spend the most time with and know the most about are the same individuals we rule out as options for companions. What does that leave us with as an option; prospective mates who we don't spend the most time with and know very little about. Does that sound dumb to anybody other than me?

What we also need to be honest about is how we treat our so called companions. What we do to our "significant others" are unthinkable actions that we don't do to our friends. Albeit illogical, there is a reason. Friendships are based on honesty, loyalty, and mutual respect, whereas most romantic relationships are based solely on eroticism, lust, aesthetic feelings and attraction. Honesty, loyalty, and respect are solid foundations that don't shake easily. Romantic feelings and attraction are flighty emotions (good, but not consistent) that crumble very easily, very often. Friendships last through rough, ugly times and we don't end friendships because we argue too much or disagree too much. We recognize that a friendship that ends so easily isn't worth having. Look at the difference between the resilience of romantic vs. plutonic relationships and we will realize that most couples are not friends. They are merely acquaintances with romantic or sexual ties. When those romantic or sexual ties get stressed and twisted estranged partners go their separate ways. Some of us don't even like the person we are intimate with. It's purely an association based on attraction and eroticism. When the attraction is gone and the eroticism turns to disinterest, the relationship turns into a painful affair. Relationships that add eroticism and attraction to friendship last. We are not in the days where relationships stay together because of fear of public opinion or for the sake of tradition or pride. Those forces kept couples together "in spite of," but they didn't keep them happy. Friendship keeps relationships together "because of" and serves as a means of maintaining happiness. Friends believe that their purpose and cause is to uplift and support one another and be there for each other when everyone else has turned their backs. That kind of interaction builds hope and happiness.

Friendship also has more accountability. We don't walk up to our friends one day and say, "I don't want to be your friend anymore because I don't feel friendly." We don't say, "I don't know why or when it happened, but I just stopped being your friend." That's unacceptable. But we will look our "loved ones" in the face and say, "I don't love you anymore and I don't know when or why I stopped. I just know I did." This lie has become a common and acceptable excuse. Not that we handle these situations well and think they are okay, but we do believe that their words are in fact representative of a real situation, that actually happened. Then we want to know why. As if love is a favorite piece of clothing we get in and out of depending on our mood. That's not love, that's like. That's not dedication, that's passing time.

Friends and relatives ask how my marriage is going all the time. I always reply that it's great, I'm happy, and that I wouldn't trade it for the world. Their next question is how long I think this (meaning all the happiness and contentment) will last. I tell them forever to which they wonder how I can be so sure. I'm sure because we work at being happy everyday and because we didn't have the luxury of attraction, eroticism, and love to cover our faults and issues with each other. For four years we were friends out of a mutual respect and appreciation for who we were and what we brought into being. I found value in her based on who she was and not who she was to me and vice versa. Even when I am upset with her I respect her and value who she is and the strength and sanctity of our relationship. When we hit rough times I am as interested in her well being as I am mine and am ever present to the commitment I have to her as her best friend. I can't afford to consider walking away because I'm fed up or frustrated or because we don't see eye to eye, because I value what we have too much to give up on her, on me, and on us. I love her as my friend and my wife. I gave her my word that I would always be there for her and I'm keeping my word. That's what friends do.

If there is an issue with dating friends it is because we haven't accepted the role friendship has in romantic relationships. We are still trying to separate the two when they aren't supposed to be separated. Changing the way we view time and friendship will change the nature and quality of our relationships and make them healthier, stronger, and longer. What I ask of all of us now is that we revisit our values and beliefs about friendships and romantic interest and make sure that they are worth hanging on to. Ensure that they are not adversely affecting our ability to maintain the kind of relationships we long for. We are obligated to come to an understanding of what we believe and why for the purpose of truly evaluating the principles we live by. Inevitably we will have to part ways with some lifelong habits and ways of being if we want to live a more fulfilled life. Letting go will not be easy but it will be necessary if we are to transform our lives from the caterpillar into the butterfly.

Cooking

We have put in an abundance of work and right now is where it all comes together. The preparation, the budgeting, the shopping, and the cleaning were all done to get to this point. We've reached the point where we take all the different elements and turn them into one delicious product that we can enjoy and be nourished by. All the other processes we went through were necessary, but don't mix them up for the entire process of cooking. All we have done is brought the food home and taken out the pots and pans. Now it is time to cook the meal. The preparation that is needed before a relationship is as much work as the relationship. Don't get caught up in the "Mc Relationship" syndrome where we expect to pull up to a drive through window and order the perfect relationship to go and get straight to eating. Unless our relationships are produced by fast food companies there is no happily-ever-after value meal. There is no act of cutting corners to save time. Get all the ingredients together, make sure your pots and pans are clean and in their proper places, and that your kitchen is clean. Put on your aprons and let's get our chef on. To eat we have to master the art of cooking.

The first step is to unwrap the food. Cooking food in plastic paper or metal sounds as nasty as it tastes. Yuuuuuck!!! To be truthful this is something we all know should be done, but when it comes to relationships it is something we don't always do. I guess it's like when you buy a candy bar and get wrapped up in a conversation and then go to bite the candy only to get a mouth full of paper. Then we chuckle at ourselves and say, "Man am I stupid. I have to open it first. Duh!" However, we get so caught up in a person or the idea of being with that person that we start to eat prematurely and get a mouth full of packaging. We get a mouthful of what they appear to be and not what they are.

Unwrapping and Inspecting

To unwrap a person is to get to know them. You spend time specifically for interaction, not for romantic interest or for sexual possibilities, unless that's all both of you are in interested in. If such is the case, then wrap it up in a condom and get your groove on. Otherwise, bringing in these aspects of romance and sexual intercourse so early is like eating plastic, styrofoam, cardboard or metal; our systems are not equipped to digest them and they will poison us and/or make us sick. We'll end up hurt and disillusioned. When we are getting acquainted, that's not the time to put on airs or misrepresent ourselves. It's not the time to convince somebody to like or appreciate us. If we've done what we were supposed to do to get to this point, convincing someone to accept, love, be attracted to, and or appreciate us will be unnecessary and out of place.

Look at the food we're about to cook and make sure it is indeed what it is supposed to be. Just like the food we buy in a grocery store can be messed up, so can the person we've just met. We could be talking to a preacher with no morals or a person with a gigantic income and no money. We could be talking to a virgin who has had more partners then they can count, so to make sure they are what they claim to be we inspect them. This is not a point of judgment it's one of verification. The purpose is not to catch someone in a lie, but to make sure they're living in the truth.

If you're dating a man who is spiritual, talk to him about his activities and what role they play in his life. After he's done talking look at his life and see if it tells you the same story. If you're talking to someone who says they're an activist down for a certain cause ask them about the cause, the place it has in their life, and how it affects their relationships. If they have no prior causes or perspectives about their place, don't fool yourself into thinking you will be the first cause they dedicate themselves to that will find a place within their lives. The key to unwrapping someone is to have and show a genuine interest in whom and what they're about. By being involved in their lives we will become familiar with what they can and can't do and what they do and don't practice. I can hear the questions now, "Why not just ask them and get it over with?" Have you ever questioned your food, asked milk if it really came from cows, or spinach whether it has all the nutrients it's supposed to have? If so how did it work out for you? I know how it worked out for your shrink.☺ Food doesn't talk and neither does a person who is presenting themselves as something they're not. Don't ask them ask their lives. Lives are like labels that can't lie; they tell you exactly what's inside. Read them carefully.

The key to unwrapping someone is to have and show a genuine interest in whom and what they're about.

If you find that the food was mislabeled or isn't what you thought it was, wrap it up, return it, and go shopping again. The time you'll invest in getting what you want will be more satisfying and fruitful than the time you would take to try to "make something work." My mother would also tell me, "Until you are married there is no such thing as 'making it work.'" If something is broke or faulty when you buy it, why in the name of all common and good sense would you try to make it work? Take it back and get what you want. You can spend time trying to turn water into wine if you want to, as for me that's not my specialty.

For all of us who have what we went shopping for the final part of unwrapping is making sure that the person you've gotten to know is on the same page as you. The point where there is an established friendship and respect between both of you is where you begin to discuss if there is a desire on both parts to add intimacy to the relationship. This conversation(s) should be honest and free. It should simply be an inquiry.

Unlike food, individuals have to agree to be part of the cooking process or it doesn't work. The way I negotiate the conversation is to let it be known that the love, appreciation, desire, or longings I have are based on who they are and therefore won't change based on how they react to them. My feelings are mine and I accept full responsibility for them. Then I let them know what the relationship means to me, no melodramatics here, I use the simple truth. *You satisfy everything I need and I want in a woman and if at any time you feel the same way about me as a man I would like the chance to have a romantic relationship with you. If you never feel the same about me we will still be the great friends we are and I will always be here for you when you need me.* At times I was told that my desire was uncomfortable and that she (the woman I was addressing) felt I was putting pressure on her. I would explain to her that I was being honest and keeping the lines of communication open and clear. If she thought I was digging her on an intimate level but was trying to hide it she still would have been uncomfortable and distrusting of my motivations. I told her that this way she would know and understand me, that I was in full control of myself and that my feelings would only affect our relationship if she let them. The end result, I am friends with some great women who I was attracted to at one time but did not try to force or coerce into a relationship they didn't want. I'm also not in contact with some of the women, but in every case what I always am is a man who walked away with the respect of the woman I was dealing with.

The goal is not to get what we want as individuals. The goal is to get what is in the best interest of both persons involved. The offering should not be an ultimatum or a demand. The last thing you want to do is give an ultimatum. Ultimatums are sharp and dangerous. If there is agreement then move to the next step, if not it's time to go shopping again.

The goal is not to get what we want as individuals. The goal is to get what is in the best interest of both persons involved.

Eating Undercooked Food

One of the most important cooking processes is to ensure that we don't undercook the food. Our anticipation of what's to come can get us into trouble if we let it influence us into hurrying along the process. We commonly call this process of under cooking premature feelings. What is a premature feeling? Who said that feelings are, or do, mature? When considering the idea or concept of feeling, where is, and who set, the standards for how much a person should or shouldn't feel in a given space of time? How emotionally attached should someone be based on a given set of circumstances? The last I checked feeling and feelings are reactions resulting from contact. You touch sand paper and it feels rough. You touch cotton and it feels soft. You meet someone nice and you like them. You meet someone mean and you dislike them. What you're feeling now is not the same as cooking. It is only cooking when you begin to prepare the meal based on those feelings. You are simply choosing your pots and pans. Your feelings in both situations are valid.

The same is true when feelings form "overnight." They are real feelings based on real situations. Am I saying that feelings intensify based solely on present situations and circumstances and the person involved, no. Every feeling we have is based on all we've experienced in life. If a woman grew up without a father figure she might become enraged easily by a man who doesn't see his children or respect family. The same woman might become immediately emotionally involved with a good man for the opposite reasons. In both cases neither feeling is premature, these feelings have formed extensively over 20 or more years. Are any of the feelings wrong? No, they're feelings. They're doing what they're supposed to do, feel. What might be "premature," to keep with the terminology, are the actions that accompany them. Eating the meal based solely on how you feel, instead of when it is fully prepared is how you undercook your relationship.

For the most part, we are taught that we are somewhat servants of our emotions. If you feel sad, cry. If you feel pain, scream. If you feel anger, release your rage. If you feel passionate, express it to the focus of your desire. None of these ideas seem harmful, but they can be if taken as "law" instead of "suggestion." How you act when emotions arise should be based on the situation not the emotion felt. No matter how much you love a thief, you should never give him the keys to your house or car. You'll end up homeless and walking. If this series of unfortunate events does happen, does it mean the love or feelings involved were premature? Nope. The action of giving away the keys is premature. Love doesn't force stupidity or bad judgment. We usually act stupid because we have not taken the time to master the balance between emotion and intellect, so to rid us of any responsibility for our actions we blame the emotion. "I was blinded by desire." Untrue, you were so happy to have someone that turned you out that you were willing to risk your entire behind to keep from messing it up. You were willing to eat the food before it was done out of fear of it never being ready to eat. You knew the risks you were taking and didn't care. I've never met someone who didn't see it coming; only those who didn't believe it was happening.

Secret Ingredients

Love doesn't force stupidity or bad judgment. We usually act stupid because we have not taken the time to master the balance between emotion and intellect, so to rid us of any responsibility for our actions we blame the emotion.

Two things usually change actions, the conscious choice to change them or an extreme situation that forces us to deal honestly with ourselves. Most of us will say we prefer change by choice rather than circumstance, but that's not how most of us operate. Most of us wait until circumstances force us to change. For example, many Americans are struggling with weight issues. They know the health risks and the dangers of overeating, but they continue their behavior. In many instances, it is not until they get a viable threat from their doctor, or become incapacitated that they jump into a change. I believe a major reason for this inability to change without extremes is we really don't understand what we are doing. Our language and terminology has gone from figurative to literal based on our continual use of it and now we have to redefine our speech to understand where we need to redefine our points of view.

Some might say I'm arguing syntax, being overly picky about words. I say words in some cases are just as important as the thought they represent. Think about the law, and contracts, and job descriptions. What if when dealing with either someone told you, "Don't worry about what it says, we both know what we mean." We all we would look at the guy like he had lost his mind. In all of these cases the wording is everything.

Whether we believe it or not the same is true of what we say.

We speak our minds and our hearts. When we say we have a "white" friend or "black" friend we have a preoccupation with color, otherwise we would just refer to them as friends. Even if the preoccupation is with society's preoccupation with color, it's still a preoccupation. So when we blame feelings or label them as premature we attack them, the way a stylist does an "ugly duckling," with the intent of making them over, making them better, and more appealing. The issue I have with labeling feelings premature is once you logically alter feelings they are no longer feelings, they're thoughts. Once the change happens you become either robotic or erratic and lose one of the most important nuances humans have, the ability to experience life through their senses and their spiritual instinct. This dulling of our emotions directly affects our ability to cook.

Feelings are wonderful things. They keep us in touch with the spiritual part of us, a part of us that communes with the world on a different level, that transcends intellect and reason. Our tendency to allow ourselves to be consumed by our emotions is not the fault or responsibility of our feelings. It is our duty to create that balance. We are as much ethereal creatures as we are carnal and both sides must be nurtured and experienced for us to truly experience peace and contentment. There are no premature feelings only premature actions. Be mindful of not eating undercooked food.

Cooking

By now we have unwrapped the food and found it is ready to be cooked. Cooking is when two individuals have come together for the purpose of preparing a relationship that both can be nourished by and enjoy. Cooking is a conscious effort to create a relationship of substance. Cooking is where two individuals have formed an agreement on what is being prepared. So the first step in the actual cooking is for you and your partner to decide what kind or relationship you are building and what the foundation of it will be. Both of you should let your expectations be known, of yourselves and each other. My wife and I based our relationship on God, Family, and the betterment of our people. When there is an issue we need to address, those are the places we return to. They act as reminders and anchors. When you establish this foundation make sure it's strong enough to support your dreams and desires because when it crumbles so does your relationship.

Anthony C. Rucker

Once you've established a foundation you turn up the heat and begin bonding your lives together. The foundation has to be whole and complete, so before you can set the foundation discuss your "non-negotiables" and "immovables." These are aspects of our lives such as spirituality, value systems, and dreams that if compromised will change who and what we are. Every one of us has them and must be honest about them.

For me I have a few. My spirituality and relationship with God are forever a part of my life and anything that would require me to sacrifice or compromise either is not happening, even if it's a relationship with the richest, most beautiful, woman on the planet. Poetry is another immoveable. Poetry is not only what I do, but is a part of who I am and I will dedicate time to reading and writing it forever. If I gave up either I would be a different person. One of my other non-negotiables is fidelity. Once it's violated I'm done. I live by word and expect the same of anyone I'm in a committed relationship with and at the time they break their word, in regards to being faithful, the relationship is over. No questions. No discussion. Though these immoveables might not seem reasonable or right to you they are still mine and still vital to who I am.

Identify what yours are. We cannot throw these non-negotiables and immoveables on the bargaining table. If we do, later in life we will blame our partners for our unhappiness and our inability to be ourselves. All our sacrifices will weigh on us so heavy we'll feel our only recourse is to throw our problems on the shoulders of who we feel is responsible for them.

Take a simple situation where a man stops hanging with his friends on Sundays to watch sports because his woman thinks it's childish. Although he has kept this tradition for the past ten years, he reluctantly gives it up to satisfy her. Later in the relationship he starts to feel like he can't do simple tasks and acts that make him happy and believes that she is the cause. When his frustrations arise he blames her and lashes out at her when he should be angry with himself for giving up a tradition that was seemingly childish to her, but of major importance to him.

Every part of our lives is not up for discussion or negotiation. Some aspects are set in stone and are not going anywhere. Keep them safe from the bargaining table or you'll bargain yourself into non-existence and unhappiness. This doesn't mean you can hide all your irrational behaviors in the nonnegotiable pile. Where there is no truth there won't be a healthy and whole relationship. Be honest about what has to stay and what can go; using honesty during this process will mean that coming together won't be self-sacrifice.

Here is the place where you discuss your individual dreams and desires for your lives and come up with a plan for them to coexist and flourish. The key is finding where your two goals intersect and understanding how they compliment each other. I'm an artist and educator and my wife is an educator and entrepreneur. My goal is to make functional art that changes the way we live our lives and set new standards for the genres I use. My wife's goals are to build a school, raise children, and to revolutionize publishing. Both of our goals are time consuming and demand intense focus and dedication. The easy way for us to achieve our dreams is for one of us to work and support the other until they reach their goal then switch roles and do it again. The problem with this method is dreams can be long and drawn out and waiting just to start one can be heartbreaking and demoralizing. So we set it up in stages. We both work for each other focusing on one project at a time. The money and connections from my success feeds hers, then hers feeds mine and vice versa until we get where we want to go. By alternating focus we support and replenish each other on a regular basis. I could always argue that my earning potential is great and therefore my projects should take precedence, but that would be a selfish fallacy.

Our relationship and its health take precedence and the earning potential of two happy supportive persons will always be greater than the potential of one unhappy person. I say unhappy because in a marriage each other's happiness is intricately intertwined and it's almost impossible for one to maintain it by him/her self.

Using this model neither of us sacrifices dreams or goals to be with the other. You could call this the cooperative dream and economic stage of the relationship. It's also where you come up with a group plan for parenting- if marriage and children are a part of your goals. Discuss the role of mother and father, how you want the children raised and how you will or won't introduce spirituality. My wife and I talked about the age our children will date and their perspective occupations. You don't have to go that far, but these will be things the two of you will eventually talk about.

What's happening during this period of cooking is the adding of the different ingredients. If you were making spaghetti sauce, you might start with tomato paste and tomato sauce then add green peppers, and maybe throw in a diced onion. That's what you're doing now, adding ingredients that will improve the health and flavor of the meal. Get to know each other's sexual character and expectations. Go over every aspect, from favorite position to kinky fantasies and dispositions. If you are getting involved with a prude or a freak that's something you need to know from the beginning. What having this information does is give you insight on how to season the relationship (we'll get to seasoning in a minute). Pet peeves are important to discuss as well. You want to know what irritates and bothers one another. Nothing is too small or too big, from favorite color to most intimate secret, depending on the depth of your relationship. You don't want to share lifelong secrets with someone who you don't plan on being with forever. Let down your guard and defenses and explore each other in your fullness. When you let the walls down it helps to cook the relationship evenly inside and out. Now we're getting someplace. The food is cooking and smelling great. Garlic is rising in the steam. Green peppers and onions are melting into the tomato sauce and chasing the garlic to our noses. The spaghetti sauce in turning into the finger-licking masterpiece we want it to be. We're happy and optimistic. Sooner or later it will get to a point where we have to let the relationship simmer.

Simmering

Simmering is when all the ingredients are mixed together and need time to sit over a low fire and absorb into each other, so their individual flavors can take on one unique taste. To simmer a relationship is to take all the conversations and beliefs you've discussed with your prospective mate and get a working knowledge of them. You have to process what you've learned. Many of us lose our way by moving too quickly. We think because we understand what was said then we understand what was meant. So off we run to act on this new found information only to find out we didn't understand everything involved. If the ingredients of the relationship are worth talking about, they're worth considering and processing and taking our time. Simmer your love. Let it sit undisturbed on low heat and work itself out. Take this time to go on dates, play, watch TV and read books. Go bike riding, to the theatre, the movies, whatever. Take these small occasions to work out how you interact. Don't immediately throw yourselves into deep and involved situations. That's the equivalent of serving food before it's ready and expecting it to taste good. Take your time. Serve the food only when it is ready.

Once our food has simmered for a good amount of time the moment has come to taste test it. For us this means evaluating the relationship; the quality, strength, character and level of it in relation to the purpose and foundation you've set. Look at the goals you've set together and where you are in regards to those goals. Figure out what you need to do to reach your destination. You might need to simmer some more or you might need to season.

Anthony C. Rucker

Seasoning

Seasoning is tweaking the food to our tastes by adding spices and flavor enhancers that weren't part of the ingredients list, like adding basil to our spaghetti sauce. We season by making the relationship more reflective of our personal tastes. If your partner likes you dressed scantily, seasoning would be dressing sexy for them during times of intimacy. If there is talk of marriage, seasoning would be adding monogamy to solidify your commitment to it. If both of you are habitually busy, seasoning would be creating a set schedule where time is set aside for quality time and it takes priority over everything. It might be as simple as giving someone personal time. Fine tune your relationship to your needs and desires.

When I come home from work I need 20 to 25 minutes of "me time" to unwind, shake off the day, and to transition into the affairs of the home. I told my wife and she understood and gave me that room. So I come home, give her a kiss and tell her I love her. Then I go off to unwind. The other seasoning we used in this situation was acknowledgement. No matter how tired or desperate for down time I was, I could never let that stand in the way of me greeting and showing appreciation for my wife. This display of respect and affection enhanced the appreciation we have for each other. That's what seasoning does; it enhances what's already there.

Don't use spices to cover up unappealing behaviors or unhealthy attitudes, it's a futile task. You'll successfully cover up the taste, but the effect it has on your system will remain. Consider this scenario of food that's so sweet it shocks your mouth and turns your stomach. To make it more palatable you add salt. The sweetness that will turn your stomach is still there. The only difference now is that you can't tell by how it tastes, but it will still turn your stomach.

We are nearing the point where we finally get to eat. We have been diligent in preparing our shopping lists, going shopping, cleaning our kitchens and choosing and preparing the proper pots and pans. We are almost ready to set the table and partake in the meal, but there are a couple of habits that might mess up the meal if we are not careful. Let's review them to make sure we keep our meal healthy and tasty.

Dipping in the Pot: Playing Married

Premarital relationships are looking more like marriages, minus the commitment, finality, and name change. Even dating has become an adventure in monogamy. Two weeks into the dating process questions arise about "who else are you seeing, are we a couple, are you willing to be faithful, etc.?" Before we are familiar with each other we are discussing the possibility of being together. Before love is present we ask for an exclusive vow of dedication and offer intercourse as incentive. I always ask the question, after two weeks of knowing and dating someone would you give them keys to your house and car, access to your bank accounts and ATM codes, and use of all of your personal belongings? Hell no! That's what we would say. But in two weeks we will give that same person full use of and access to our bodies, thereby entrusting them with our emotional and physical well being, and exclusive rights to our fidelity and intimacy. How does that work; that we will take more time in deciding about, and precaution regarding the use of our possessions than we will over the use of our very selves? *Take my body whenever you want, but leave my car alone.* Sounds funny doesn't it, but that's what we are saying with our actions. We put more value on and assign a greater cost to what we own than who we are. Quit lying to yourself, yes you do. Dipping in the pot also eliminates the uniqueness and meaning of marriage. In some ways playing married devalues it. Not the ceremony of the wedding, but the seriousness of the vows; forgetting that the strength and security that comes with the benefits of marriage come from the permanence of those very vows.

Let's examine what the benefits without the vows really say. I'll give you love, devotion, fidelity, and even share my living space as long as you keep me happy, treat me right, and stay out of my way. If you think this an exaggeration, then ask the reverse question. Do you promise to give me devotion, fidelity and the privilege of sharing your living space forever? But you can't ask that question because it's too much like marriage vows. What playing married is tantamount to is working at a company 8 hours a day 5 days a week for a paycheck and benefits, only for the company to start paying the exact same salary and benefits to those who don't work for them. What you begin to ask yourself is, "Why am I employed if I can get paid without working?" The same questions are arising about marriage. Why do we have to be married, can't we just live together? Why do we have to exchange vows, can't we just have children? Why do we have to put stipulations or titles on our love?

The belief is, "We don't need a piece of paper to validate our love," or "We don't need the government in our business." Both of these interpretations are true, but have nothing to do with the ideal and practice of marriage. Marriage is a promise and commitment to become life partners where all is in common and breaking the relationship and vows is not an option, for better or worse, in sickness and health, till death do us part.

The beauty of relationships for most of us is not in the action, it is in the implications of the action. It's not the moving in together that's so appealing; it's the moving in with someone you love and want to share your life with who wants to do the same with you. It's not having children; it's creating children with someone you want to be the parent of your child and to establish a legacy with someone who wants the same of you. I don't know of anyone who moves in together with the hopes of breaking up, or who initially conceives a child with the desire to never see the other parent again. Even if it isn't stated, it's at least hoped or believed that these commitments will be long lasting. What I don't understand is why? If there has been no stated commitment outside of the physical act, why do we assume that one exists?

If your partner does not specifically express a desire and make an effort to create "forever" do not

---

Secret Ingredients

"We don't need a piece of paper to validate our love," or "We don't need the government in our business." Both of these interpretations are true, but have nothing to do with the ideal and practice of marriage.

create it for them. It will not make them any more or less dedicated to the relationship. Devotion is not something that can be forced or manufactured with a plethora of positive thinking; besides, most of us can't emotionally afford it when the "unconditional love check" bounces. Worlds end, hearts question whether they can love again, genders develop an unconditional distrust of the other and it happens because we weren't honest with ourselves.

The discussion of this form of self-deception illustrates the importance of other aspects of marriage, specifically the clearly defined expectations and reciprocity of your mate. Marriage takes away the need to assume and do guess work by openly stating intentions and the dedication to being faithful to them. Albeit some marry when they are not committed to it, but my views are not based on liars or the fainthearted. They are based on those who are true to their word. If you worry about the honesty of your mate, you need to reevaluate each other and your choices and not the institution of marriage. The reason it's so important to know if you are in a marriage, traditional or non-traditional, is easily seen in the exact opposite situation; two individuals who have no idea what they have and therefore have no way to make good decisions about anything, except short term goals and aspirations. But just as people grow tired of living check to check, they also grow tired of living day to day.

It's from this desire/frustration point that society has created the unmarried-married status of dating that exists now; where you can have all the signs of permanency and joint long term goals, where it appears absolution of the relationship is the very last option without ever having to commit to it or even acknowledge that the desire to commit to it exists. Couples have dated for ten years or more but refused to get married. Their reasoning, for all intents and purposes, is that they are as good as married. One of the many problems with this misconception is the fact that marriage is a confirmation of dedication, not just the act itself. As with a job, what employer would hire someone who refused to fill out an application, or refused to sign a job description form, just because they're good and hard workers and don't need such oaths or guidelines to govern their behavior? Not one, because they don't want to assume you will work; they want to know. Your mate also wants to know that you'll be around, not assume. Contrary to popular belief, other than vowing to be committed forever unconditionally, there is no action that will let someone know that you are. Not moving in nor building a house. Houses are sold everyday and people move for every notion, from jobs to weather. Buying a ring will not make the statement either; rings are symbols and only have meaning and power to those who believe in them. It isn't having children. Creating life and being willing to nurture life are two different things, besides parents abandon children every day. The only way to know there is "forever" is if you let someone know there is a "forever" and honor those words.

At the risk of being ostracized I have to ask, If you don't plan to marry the person you're in a monogamous relationship with why do you limit yourself to dating only them? Why make a long term commitment when there is no long term desire. If the ultimate goal is to find someone to spend the rest of your life with, why give exclusive rights to someone you only want to spend your life with right now? That seems like selling your car for gas money. One rationale I've heard is that it takes time to get to know someone. I don't know what that has to do with monogamy. The real issue is intimacy and impatience. We want to be intimate on the level of a dedicated couple before we are a couple and want the security of knowing that that privilege isn't being shared by another. Our "getting to know" is really "getting involved." Again, we want to be married when we are not married.

The other problem playing married presents is that of the "other woman/man" when there is no other woman/man. Outside of marriage, nothing's guaranteed. Anyone can leave anybody at any time for any reason, and unless it was stated that you are "the one" there can't be "another one." You're all just a bunch of maybes who want to be the one. If you don't believe me ask your significant other and see what they have to say.

I've witnessed in many cases, situations where someone meets the person of their dreams, who they can't date because of their current relationship. The desire to leave one for the other arises, but that is not politically correct. So the desire to creep arises, that way you appear p.c. and get to have what you think is best for you. Two problems, you live a lie and build a shaky foundation for your "perfect" relationship. The final outcome is you let that dream-mate go and later your relationship ends anyway; where if you had waited until you met your dream-mate you could have avoided the whole mess and at least been committed to someone you planned on being with for the long term.

There are many issues that we use to cloud our judgment and justify our way of acting, but anyway you slice it, playing married is not healthy. Either you are unconditionally dedicated or you're not. Either you are married or your not. There's no in between or half way. Like pregnancy and death. Marriage is definite and absolute.

Relationship Cookbook

Marriage is definite and absolute.

Playing With Knives

Playing with knives is the quickest way to injure ourselves by cutting off a finger or putting out an eye. For that reason we should be careful about how we handle them and if we're not, we'll pay for it. For her birthday, I bought my wife a knife set from an infomercial. They were advertised as the sharpest knife set in the world with a lifetime guarantee. When we got them home she couldn't wait to use them. She was in the kitchen for all of three minutes before I heard a yell. My wife had cut her finger. Three minutes later she yelled again, she had cut herself again. Finally I asked her what she was doing that she was cutting herself so much. She said the knives were so sharp that just touching the blade was cutting her. I told her not to handle those knives like the duller ones she was used to or she was going to be fingerless in a week. Once she started being more careful she stopped cutting herself.

As a rule we should handle sharp objects with care to avoid hazardous situations. In most cases we avoid them all together and only pull them out when we need them. This rule of thumb helps us minimize the chances of us needlessly getting hurt. Minimizing hurt is a good thing especially when it comes to our feelings and mental health. Therefore it is important to avoid sharp objects that can mentally and emotionally scar us. We should use them only when necessary and as infrequently as possible.

As with being physically cut, being cut in our hearts and minds is hard to forget and leaves a visible mark that makes it easy to remember. But, bruising has not stopped us from carving each other up like a thanksgiving turkey. Some of has have went Jack the Ripper on numerous occasions. I don't know if it's because we don't know or just don't care about what we're doing. Either way we need to become fully cognizant of the effects of our actions. First we need to be able to recognize sharp items. The act of recognition seems so simple, but based on current events I guess it isn't. Here is a list of sharp knives that we need to exercise better use of.

Criticism. Do I need to expound? Used as a habitual means of communication, it will kill positive communication and self esteem. In most cases we mistake it for critique or advice. "I'm going to tell him about himself, I'm going read her from head to toe." When we get in that mode of thinking we're not being constructive, we're being destructive. We're tearing someone down because we don't like them or appreciate them. But dig this, tearing down a broken down building doesn't guarantee someone will build a new one. The only thing guaranteed is there will be rubble and ruin. That's how we leave each other when we criticize, ruined; there is no guarantee we will be anything else. Sometimes we go off and run down a person's list of faults. We walk away thinking we've done some kind of service and expect circumstances to have changed next time we see them. When we find nothing has changed we make character judgments and assume that person is only interested in staying the messed up creature they are, but as with destroying a building if we want a newer prettier one in its place we have to build it. The building is not going to build itself or appear by magic. Breaking down someone teaches them how to fall not how to get up. Once you take what someone has then help them to get what they need to rebuild. Believe it or not some of us are not conscious of why we do what we do and need help rectifying our ways. When we help build someone up we are critiquing. Unless we critique we have no reason to expect change. Don't expect to see rebuilding when all you are doing is destroying.

Ultimatums. In war there is a rule. Always give your enemy a means of escape because if cornered their only way out is through you. The nature of a person changes when they run out of options. The most dangerous kind of enemy to deal with is one who has nothing to lose. A cornered person is no different. When we give ultimatums we put others in a corner and allow them only one exit, through or over us. Their nature changes to strictly survival and self-preservation. This desperation builds tension and animosity. It also builds the belief that for one to be happy the other has to go. Before we know it a simple situation has turned into a chaotic free-for-all where everyone ends up being hurt. Using ultimatums for anything except a last resort is a recipe for unhappy times and painful breakups.

Withholding Sex. I personally hate this one! Sex is one of the sharpest knives in the drawer. We associate it with our confidence and attractiveness, self-esteem, desire for our significant other, and physical expression of emotions. When we deny access to sex we bottle up all these aspects of ourselves and put our partners in a very precarious position where their only choice is to give in to our demands or explode. This is just an ultimatum in lingerie, or silk boxers, depending on your gender preference. Like ultimatums, with-holding sex has the same result. Using sex as a tactic cheapens it by reducing it to a bargaining chip. It is now seen as a means to an end instead of a sacred expression and act. Kind of like a scooby-snack. We get them when we are good or when someone wants us to carry out a specific act. At this point sex becomes mechanical and totally self-serving. Who knows when the next time will be, so the goal is to get as much out if it for ourselves as humanly possible.

Ignoring or Purposefully Forgetting. No matter the intention this act is selfish and cold. Whether or not we are friends with our mates there is still a basic amount of trust we have in them. When we ignore or purposely forget to be responsible to each other we are blatantly breaking that trust. When a trust is broken between two persons it chips away at the foundation of their union. There is an assumption that by ignoring someone they will get the point and react accordingly, but truth be told most people don't understand why they are being ignored and take this as a sign of ill will and contempt. Unless we clearly express our discontent we can't expect others to be aware of it. We have this belief that what we feel is so right and obvious and what someone has done is so wrong and easy to see that our silence or neglect couldn't be because of or mistaken for anything else. So we wait for the proper response to our protest and until we get it we are some cold uncaring so-and-so's. I don't know why we think this kind of immature petty behavior will bring about any positive results. As far I know most of us are not psychic and therefore mind reading is not our strong suit. If you expect someone to read your mind, write down what you're thinking and give it to them. That's the only way it's going happen on a regular basis.

Jealousy. Sometimes we like it when our significant other gets aggravated because someone is obviously attracted to us and is giving us a whole lot of attention. Doesn't it make you feel desirable when two interested parties are battling for you? Flirting and making eyes at strangers solicits reactions that let us know someone cares. It makes for a great story to tell our friends and is a big boost to our self-confidence. It also brings out a volatile part of our mate's psyche that is usually irrational and angry. When we react as if our need to be desired is validated and fulfilled by this show of jealousy guess what are partners are thinking? They're thinking that this is the only way to satisfy us and that they're constantly being challenged and expected to prove their love for us in that way. We've successfully created the perfect green eyed monster, but like in every monster movie the monster eventually becomes too much for its creator. The creator then has to choose between destroying the monster and being destroyed. Play this game at your own risk, especially if you're black. Everybody knows all the black people get killed in monster movies.

Using Love like Money. How do we love? Most of us love like banks and corporations. Love is an entity that we invest in in hopes of a making a return. Not many of us love another person because of who that person is to themselves or is as a person. Most of us love someone because of who they are to, and what they do for, us. Ask the question, "Why do you love him or her?" and you'll hear, "They're good to me. They make me smile. They make me laugh. They understand me. I can trust them." Almost all of these answers we hear are based on the relationship between the couple and not on who the person is in relation to him/her self. I can hear it now, "So, what's the matter with that?" Answer, a whole lot. Our love for another person should not be based on how much they appease us or appeal to us. That's what "like" is for. When we "like" someone it's based on how we feel a particular day or about a particular characteristic, it's flighty, unstable, and it leaves no materials in which to build a relationship of any kind off of.

Love is supposed to go beyond the fickle self and look at the foundation of a person and see them for who and what they really are. It is the ability to see the diamond even when it is partially formed under a pile of dirt and understand the value of it. Not to say love is supposed to mine the diamond or be responsible for its formation, but love has the ability to recognize the presence and process of diamonds. Once love recognizes that there is a pricelessness about a person it doesn't seek to own or control or monopolize it. It seeks communion and the experience of the beautiful, and if there is reciprocity then the two love one another, and if there's mutual agreement then the love that binds two people intimately together is made into a bond exclusively for them. Contrary to popular belief love doesn't love to be loved, it loves because it is love and that's what love does.

The way love is practiced now doesn't mirror the principle love for love's sake. We are told not to say, "I love you," until our partner is ready to say it too because it hurts when love is not reciprocated. Think about that, what we are saying is, "It hurts to love you unless you love me, and I don't want to express any love for you unless you are going to do the same for me." What if every relationship was this way: parent-to-child, teacher-to-student, and sibling-to-sibling. Until I know you love me, you won't know I love you. There would be world chaos. This principle only works in business; I won't sell the product until you have the money to buy it or I won't invest my money in this partnership until you're willing to invest yours. Once you put the expectation and demand of getting something in return on love you lose the power of it. You turn it into an ultimatum instead of an offer, a loan instead of a gift. Gifts are given to show appreciation and love, not to say, "Now you have to give me something." If they do, they're not gifts, they're investments, business ventures no different than purchasing things; the simple act of giving to get.

Playing the Guessing Game. We have been programmed to expect a return on our love, gifts, and affection, but have also been programmed not to voice this expectation because it's not proper. We turn relationships into a game of charades acting out clues until our partners guess them (finally "fall in love") or time runs out (they never figure it out and the game is over). That sucks!!!

There is a simple word we use everyday but hardly ever put into good use, communication. Businesses don't allow personal communication when it comes to buying or selling their stocks, its called insider trading. All you discuss is the overt, obviously seen aspects of the public relationship. This scene probably sounds like most of our relationships. Never reveal insider secrets until we are ready to form a merger: we are both willing to commit. We refuse to reveal our insider secrets for the same reasons as businesses; we think it makes us vulnerable and it's not safe. What we fail to recognize is that our fear and vulnerability is solely based on our expectations and desires for a return on our investment. If I wasn't worried about someone loving me back I would never have a problem with saying I love you first. If there wasn't the expectation of reciprocation or implied ownership people wouldn't freak out or run away when someone told them they loved them. It would be an understanding that he/she sees something wonderful in me and is willing to acknowledge it by loving me. When a child expresses love to a parent there isn't an anxiety or fear, it's a joy to know that someone loves you and finds you worth loving. The mother doesn't freak out and say, "Now my child owns me."

My father told me about a conversation he had with a woman he dated. She told him he was amazing because he never changed in the way he treated her. When she was flaky he was as consistent as he was when she wasn't flaky. She really didn't understand it. My father told her he never changed because she never changed. What he meant was she was still the same person he loved. He also said that his love for her wasn't based on their relationship with one another, but based on his love for her.

Going on he explained that when she acted flaky the only element that changed was the nature of the relationship. When she started acting funny he backed up and gave her some distance. He still let her know he was there for her, but would not support the madness she was creating. When she needed an ear or a hand he was still there, nonjudgmental, encouraging, and loving. Simply said, "I don't need you to love me for me to love you or to acknowledge it." It was a choice he'd made, not an obligation or an investment. For that reason his expectations and actions were different than men she had dated before. What also struck me in this story was that love didn't mean becoming a victim or losing your ability to reason. You don't have to subjugate yourself to wearing someone's burdens, just be there when they need you to help them carry their cross, listen to their pain, or find encouragement. It didn't mandate suffering, abuse and humiliation; it was alright to say "I'll hug you, but I won't let you hit me. I love you, but that doesn't mean you can abuse me."

Uniformed Consumer. Another part of our capitalistic nature that arises is that of the uninformed consumer. For the most part we believe if we have enough money to buy something we should be able buy it regardless of whether or not we can afford it or if it's good for us. This is how most of us shop for mates; if I'm good enough to get a certain person then I should be able to have them. If they look good and are well off they are a good catch. All these bad shopping habits usually result in high debt, extreme stress, counseling of some sort, and some form of debt consolidation. We overspend. We give more of ourselves than we have to spare because "it's worth it." What we lose of our self respect or personal resolve will be justified once we hook that special person. We'll be able to replace the money we spent because the relationship will be so beautiful that we'll be rejuvenated and justified. We'll live happily ever after and forget how we sold ourselves to get what we wanted. The end result is usually a feeling of regret. We become regretful that we spent so much time on something we really didn't want or need, and now want so desperately to get rid of, but have so much invested in. Where, if we had used our better judgment we would have most likely never ended up in that situation in the first place. Just as we are told to learn good money management skills we should learn good time and judgment managing skills. We need to learn the value of who we are and what we do, so that we won't throw them away so carelessly. If you don't balance time you will waste it, and if you don't respect judgment you will suffer the fate of fools.

Most people don't save money. Most people don't save themselves. They splurge because tomorrow is not promised. When tomorrow gets here they end up taking out loans to make it through today. They'll totally submerge themselves in a relationship not having fully assessed the risks and lose everything or give it all away. Then they'll call in loans, long conversations with friends, extensive periods of isolation to work through the pain, counseling, refusing to be involved in a relationship, emotional trauma, etc. These loans come at the price of our peace of mind, stability, and ability and desire to love. You end up taking from one part of your life to repair another and sometimes mess up the only parts you were happy about. Here is the true meaning of debt, when you have to pay yourself for what you've lost of yourself. There isn't an efficient way to refinance your heart or to make payments on your soul. If there is a "most precious" commodity on earth it is the human self and it should be used accordingly.

There are so many ways that our relationships mimic capitalism, the key to getting over this habit is close attention to detail. Ask yourself honest questions. Am I treating my relationship like a commodity? Am I spending emotions like money? Am I acting more like I'm starting a relationship or a corporation? Am I investing time or enjoying someone's company? Am I making a down payment or building a friendship? Questions similar to these will help you refocus and identify how you are really approaching your relationships. What we put in is what we get out, and it is important to know what exactly we are putting in.

The list of sharp objects is extensive and can't be listed in its entirety; however playing with sharp objects is a subject we need to be thorough in exploring. Make a list of knives that can damage or destroy your relationship and how they destroy. Read and re-read the list and become overly familiar with what they are and how they should be handled. If you need to, practice and role play with friends. Create adverse situations and become conscious of how you react and what utensils you use when you do. You might have a habit of playing with sharp objects that you don't know about. In the end I say safety first! Be as careful with other's feelings as you would be handling a very sharp knife.

Once the meal is cooked to the satisfaction of both of you then you get to set the table and get ready to eat.

Setting the Table

Setting the table is preparing your lives to receive the relationship and its commitments in a supportive and healthy environment. If we're about to move in with someone setting the table would be deciding where we're going to live, what furniture we would keep, the rules of the house, finding out any special demands we have about our living space, what we expect the house to look like, how we expect it to function, and each other's personal responsibilities. By making these specifications known, we create a space for the relationship to grow and mature. Consider what setting the table would look like for your relationship and apply the necessary tactics. Once the table is set the meal can now be served.

*Relationship*Cookbook

Believe it. We have prepared an extremely healthy and tasty meal. It is a meal created in the best interest of both persons eating and is seasoned to fit all parties' particular tastes. We have meticulously put in the effort and time necessary to be deserving of a great relationship. We have done the shopping, the cleaning, the inspecting, practiced kitchen safety, and set a glorious table. The work has afforded us the meal of our dreams. Applaud yourself for loving you enough to take extra special care of you. Now we finally get to eat what we have worked so hard to prepare.

Congratulations on cooking a great meal!

Eating

Bon Appétit! Chow Down! Dig In! Come & Get It! Get Your Grub On! Let's Eat! Once you've reached this point you will be sitting in front of a three course gourmet, healthy, great tasting meal. All of your diligent labor was for a great tasting, healthy, fulfilling relationship, made to last a lifetime. Eating is enjoying and maintaining your delicious relationship. The goal now becomes maintaining the relationship in all its splendor and cooking glory. The key is to be consistent in doing what you did to get here. As we live and experience the different flavors and textures life has to offer we grow, modify, change, become wiser, and expand our points of view. To ensure the relationship grows, the steps in the cooking section should be repeated and tweaked to improve the taste as needed.

If we stop practicing our cooking skills, we will eventually destroy what we worked so hard to create. We cannot allow ourselves to take the relationship for granted because being indifferent will lead to bad habits. Bad habits will ensure that we will have to start the cooking process over, possibly from the very beginning. Following are two sections that will give insight on bad habits and ideas we tend to carry around like old, heavy, beat-up, once-overpriced luggage that will have negative repercussions on the relationship.

Talking With Your Mouth Full

No one wants to see what were eating after we've started chewing it but every one of us has had to tell someone to keep their mouth closed when they're chewing. All of us have said, "What did you say?" after somebody decided to talk while stuffing their faces. I think the universal opinion when someone talks with their mouth full is, "Chew first and talk later because you're spitting out food and I have absolutely no idea what you're saying." This doesn't stop anybody from doing it. The results are predictable. One person thinks they've expressed themselves clearly and the other person clearly thinks they're dealing with someone with no manners. One person thinks they've made their point and the other has no idea what the point was. The final outcome is inevitably misunderstanding because there is a false assumption that there was some sort of agreement understanding or communication made. But whatever was said lived and died inside of the unprocessed slightly chewed food. Sad to say this process is how most of us speak emotionally, with our mouths full.

When we get excited or are moved by an experience we are initially full of undigested and unprocessed thoughts and feelings. When we talk we are talking with our mouths full, showing all that nasty looking partially chewed on emotion. Our emotions become like that food that flies out of our mouths when we talk and chew at the same time. When we talk with our mouths full our words are muffled and hard to understand. When we act without logically processing our emotions they become incoherent, like gibberish that only we can understand. All the other person is hearing is crude-mashed-together words that we think make perfect sense, but only make sense to us.

This jumbled ranting usually results in someone turning away from us, or being too distracted by the harshness or incoherence of our words to pay attention to what we are attempting to say. We don't recognize that what's happening inside of us is affecting what's coming out of our mouths, what we say, and how we say it so much that we are offending or confusing the person we claim we want to communicate with. Then when they don't respond or express an understanding of what we've said we assume that they weren't listening to us or were too into what they were thinking to consider what we had to say. The truth is we expressed what we felt before we understood and could effectively express what we were feeling.

Emotions are foods that have to be digested and processed to get the proper nutrients out of them. When we are experiencing them we are chewing them and we all know that the nourishment doesn't come from chewing. It comes from swallowing and breaking down. In this stage we absorb the nutrients and get rid of the excess. We need to take time to absorb and process our feelings. At the onset of pain or discomfort our initial reaction is protection and preservation. When we get intensely happy our tendency is to over indulge and become consumed. Immediately, we begin speaking or acting on the intense happiness because of how great it feels. We are led to making statements we don't fully mean. In our lack of understanding our feelings of pain we put the person we're talking to in a position where they feel pressured, overwhelmed, and sometimes trapped. However, our exuberance can be as damaging as pain and our initial reaction should be preservation of the emotional health of all involved.

We should remove ourselves from the emotional intensity, then figure out what happened and why. I have no idea why we don't do this with our relationships. When we initially feel anything good or bad we are purely reacting to it. To speak on our feelings at this point is like trying to describe accidentally putting our hands on a hot surface before moving them away. Besides saying it's hot and screaming a lot we wouldn't be to in-depth about the description of the situation because we're still experiencing the heat and the pain. We haven't had a chance to process the situation and the emotions we're felling and put it in context with the rest of our lives and present situations. So when we get so moved by our feelings we end up making statements and or promises that we want to take back, modify, or apologize for later because they weren't true representations of how we honestly feel. If a situation arises where what you said and what the person you were talking to got out of what you said is totally different, ask yourself if you were talking with your mouth full. Replay what you said and ask yourself if what you said made sense to someone who didn't know the motivations and situations that led up to it. Ask yourself if what you said could have been truly understood by someone other than you. If your answer is maybe or no then your next step is learning how to say exactly what you mean and having the discussion again.

    We think we're not being spontaneous or we're messing up the moment when we stop to think or are not sure of what's happening in that moment. What we don't think about is that we can't take back what we say and that it's better to say what we are sure we feel later than to say what we're not sure about now. How many of us have spoken with our mouths full of our feelings only to be asked later, "What did you mean by that?" or "Did you mean it when you said . . . ?" At which point we are like, "Damn what did I get myself into?" We begin asking ourselves, "What conversation were they in?" The real question is what conversation were we in. We were so busy expressing what we weren't sure about that we created a situation that we didn't want to be a part of. We were talking and chewing at the same time and didn't properly communicate anything at all. There seems to be an immediate importance to what we want to say and so we say it while we're doing something else and thereby do the importance of our message a terrible disservice.

If what we have to say is worth saying it's worth saying in its proper context in its proper time. If the span of a few minutes, hours, or days will consume the memory and meaning of what we're feeling then what we we're feeling wasn't all that important was it? Take your time and respect what you have to say. Chew, swallow, and then speak. It will do wonders for you!

Anthony C. Rucker

Fresh vs. Spoiled Food

When we buy fruit, we make sure it is fresh and ripe, not spoiled and rotten. Before we buy perishable foods the first detail we check is the expiration date. Why, because we want to make sure it will be good when we want to eat it. If we buy apples to bake a pie in January and then change our minds and decide to wait until May, we wouldn't use the apples we bought five months ago; they would either be eaten or rotten and wilted. We would buy new ones. People want fresh food, not spoiled food. Even leftovers get old and nasty over time. This concept seems so simple and basic that it doesn't need to be stated, but for some reason we have not made this association when it comes to factors that affect our relationships. We use old, moldy, rotten, decomposed, actions and ideas and wonder why our lovers tell us we make them sick. Of course they're sick. They're suffering from food poisoning. We're stuffing them full of decomposed junk.

Mix ups about what is "fresh" and what is "spoiled" happens when we don't pay attention, get lazy, or are not interested in maintaining our current relationships. Fresh foods are new creative ideas that stimulate the taste buds of intimacy. They add flavor to romance and keep it healthy and desirable. They are the surprise visits, calls just because, rose petals spread across the bed, and love notes placed in different places for someone to find. Any one of these gestures will bring a smile to a face and warmth to a heart, but if one of them were all we did for the next forty years it would grow old real quick. The "you used to like it" statements would start to fly. Yeah they liked it the first 100 times we did it. Now the act is the same as that apple from five months ago. It's spoiled and toxic. The nutrients it used to have are gone. Using the same ideas year after year and expecting the same reaction and stimulation as we did when we first used them is where we go wrong. It ain't gonna happen! If I tried to feed you pieces of the same cake for three years would you be excited or stimulated? So why do we use ingredients that we bought years ago and get mad when our partners refuse to eat them or look at us in disgust? The flowers on Valentine's Day and anniversaries are the most common forms of spoiled food. Pretty soon our loved ones catch on to the quick fix for when we forget to get them a "real" present. To further the charade we get offended when we're called on it, acting as if we are

---

Secret Ingredients

Fresh foods are new creative ideas that stimulate the taste buds of intimacy. They add flavor to romance and keep it healthy and desirable.

being under appreciated. Knowing the whole time we are attempting to take advantage. We should be totally ashamed. Nothing's more insulting than feeding someone crap while claiming its cookies, especially when they can smell the stench from across the room. A few minutes a day reserved for picking fresh food is all we need to rectify this situation.

Creativity and consideration are the two main resources that keep food fresh and preserve them. Show you care by your words and actions. What helps me is making lists. For me some days are more creative than others, so when I'm feeling creative I come up with as many new ideas as possible. Then when I'm feeling the urge to surprise my wife I have many to choose from. I repeat ideas, of course, but it's out of choice, not necessity. Most of us repeat the same acts all the time because we haven't invested time in coming up with new ideas. Relying on "old faithful" we become boring, predicable, and unattractive. There's no excitement or freshness to us. We become stale as old potato chips. The easiest way to come up with new ideas is to use variations of old ones. For example rose petals on the bed could be replaced with pictures of special times. You'll reminisce as each picture is picked up and a specific memory is shared about each one. By the time all of the pictures are up you have a bed that is now a field of memories to make more on. Used on random and surprise occasions the bed will become a new point of anxiousness and expectations. Simple romantic measures like this will add years onto our lives.

A valuable resource is also friends. I remember times when my girlfriends used to ask me to speak to their girlfriends' boyfriends' and give them pointers. In the end all of them thanked me for it. I paid attention to everything growing up and I recall overhearing conversations of the older men talking about what women do and don't like. Most of it was on point. I know because I used most of it. Asking for advice doesn't make you any less caring or special. It makes you smart and more creative. If you are hesitant to ask for advice, read books. People have been getting busy since time's first tick, why reinvent the wheel? Study what's worked for others. It might work for you. Nothing's guaranteed, but even if you don't move mountains your partner will appreciate the effort and reward you for it nicely. They'll also give you some pointers as to what will increase their heart rate and peak their interest, which leads to the most reliable and effective way to pick fresh food; ask your significant other.

I don't mean interview them. I mean talk to them. Talk about everything from silly to serious. Find out what they're made of. Pay attention to details and write them down later if you need to. There are very few things in life that move someone more than knowing they're listened to and appreciated. If we create situations made up of the inner workings of the heart and mind, we won't have any problems getting others involved and excited. One Christmas I asked a friend to come over because I had gotten her something. She felt uncomfortable about me buying her a present because she hadn't got me one. I told her not to worry about it and to just come over. When she arrived I gave her a white ceramic Christmas tree and a card that read "to find peace of mind stare into heaven until you find God." To you these gifts probably seem insignificant. Now take into account that what she wanted for Christmas was peace of mind and what she looked forward to was getting her own house so she could celebrate Christmas by putting up a big white Christmas tree. The note attached to my gift was "use this until you can put up one of your own." Totally changes the meaning doesn't it. I listened to her in detail. She mentioned them both in passing during a two hour long conversation, but they stood out to me by the way she talked about them. Collectively she talked about both for about minute a piece, with joy and desire in her voice. I figured that she wasn't expecting either so I got her both. I did it because she was important to me and I wanted whatever I did to mean something to her.

Meaning and importance are two vital essentials to consider when picking fresh food. Creativity and consideration show you are dedicated. Meaning and importance are indicators that you care. Although we want to feel good about giving, the main goal is to make others feel good about receiving. Make them feel good by being selective and purposeful in your giving. Remember, actions like food lose their freshness and nutritional value over time. Check the expiration dates, don't be afraid to throw away spoiled food, and don't try to sneak spoiled food on the plate with the new because it will mess up both. Being diligent about checking expiration dates will keep our relationships healthy, new, and unpredictable. In a word, it will keep them fresh.

Clean Up When You're Done

Although you have cleared the table and washed your used dishes, you're definitely not at the end of our cooking session. Cooking and eating are ongoing processes that we need to practice and continue to keep our relationships alive, healthy and full of flavor. Always remember the journey you took and the transformation you've made to get to this point. Keep familiar with the entire process.

- Identifying the diet
- Cleaning the kitchen
- Making your list
- Setting a budget
- Going Shopping
- Unwrapping the food
- Cooking
- Simmering
- Seasoning
- Eating

Revisit each step as much as it becomes necessary for you. It is regular maintenance that prevents major breakdowns. It is also practicing proper cooking techniques that make us better chefs. Always keep in mind the foundation and purpose of the relationship and use its joy, love and purpose to keep all the various elements and aspects of your relationship in perspective.

Finally, eat for health & taste, enjoy life, and love freely. Love, Peace & God Bless ~~

Anthony

Acknowledgements

The author wishes to acknowledge Dr. Michael R. Williams, Marléna Rucker, Freddie Rucker, Margaret Rucker, Regie & Katie O'hare-Gibson, Earl & Patty Jenkins, Eloise P. Miller, Andrew & Lucille Butts, Pastor Ron Williams, Terrance F. Rucker, Freddie Warner, DJ Renegade, all the happily married couples who gave me advice along the way, and all the those who made me who I am.

Index

A

Attraction 109, 111

B

Balance .. 8, 24, 84, 91, 98, 123, 125, 153
Behaviors 53, 54, 95, 128, 134
Blame 22, 109, 123, 125, 127
Budget 35, 39, 171
Budgeting 35, 37, 115

C

Capitalism 56, 154
Cleaning 42, 43, 46, 47, 48, 49, 51, 52, 77, 78, 115, 134, 156, 171
Communication 120, 143, 150, 160, 163
Compromise 48, 63, 66, 127
Cooking 8, 23, 26, 29, 33, 34, 41, 42, 49, 67, 71, 78, 79, 81, 82, 83, 92, 113, 115, 116, 119, 121, 126, 130, 156, 159, 171
Cooking utensils 26
Criticism 143

D

Dipping in the pot 135
Distrust 53, 138

E

Emotions .. 23, 77, 82, 83, 84, 85, 87, 88, 90, 91, 92, 93, 94, 96, 97, 109, 122, 125, 145, 154, 161, 162, 163
Eroticism 109, 111

F

Feelings 68, 77, 85, 86, 89, 90, 104, 108, 109, 119, 121, 122, 123, 125, 143, 155, 161, 162, 163, 164
Forgetting 135, 146
Fresh food 165, 168, 170
Friends 16, 17, 20, 21, 29, 39, 59, 107, 108, 109, 110, 111, 112, 120, 125, 128, 146, 147, 153, 155, 168

G

Friendship . 87, 107, 108, 109, 110, 112, 119, 154

Guilt 22

H

Health 7, 13, 37, 56, 124, 129, 130, 137, 143, 162, 172

I

Ignoring 146
Immaturity 22
Independence 61, 62
Inspecting 116, 156
Intellect 82, 83, 85, 87, 89, 90, 91, 96, 98, 123, 125

J

Jealousy 147

K

Kitchen ... 35, 42, 46, 47, 51, 71, 86, 116, 142, 156, 171
Knives 142, 143, 145, 154

L

Lies 52
Love 7, 13, 18, 20, 22, 51, 55, 56, 60, 63, 65, 66, 70, 74, 79, 80, 84, 87, 93, 94, 96, 97, 99, 107, 108, 109, 111, 117, 119, 123, 132, 133, 135, 136, 137, 138, 147, 148, 149, 150, 151, 153, 166, 172

M

Marriage 59, 79, 111, 129, 130, 133, 135, 136, 138, 139, 140, 141, 142
Maturity 74, 76, 77, 107
Meals 34, 35, 82, 90, 91, 102
Messiah complex 73
Microwave 25, 104, 107

Money.16, 18, 37, 40, 53, 61, 62, 67, 88, 103, 117, 129, 140, 147, 149, 152, 153, 154
Myths 53

O

Opposite sex 47, 61
Ovens 98

P

Parenthood 59
Parenting 130
Playing married 135, 136, 140, 141
Playing with knives 142
Pots & Pans 81, 82, 85, 86, 87, 91, 95, 115, 122, 134

R

Relationships.. 7, 8, 9, 15, 20, 21, 23, 24, 29, 30, 32, 34, 37, 40, 43, 46, 47, 48, 55, 57, 58, 59, 61, 65, 67, 71, 77, 79, 80, 81, 89, 90, 98, 100, 102, 104, 105, 106, 108, 109, 112, 115, 116, 118, 134, 137, 150, 154, 162, 165, 170, 171
Romance 31, 107, 116, 165

S

Seasoning 130, 133, 171
Second chances 71, 72, 73

Setting the table 155
Sex 48, 59, 60, 61, 67, 70, 71, 145
Shopping .. 17, 35, 36, 37, 38, 39, 41, 42, 102, 115, 119, 121, 134, 152, 156, 171
Simmering 131, 171
Snacks 36
Spoiled food 165, 166, 170
Stereotypes 7, 21, 47, 95
Superficial treats 36
Superstitions 100, 101

T

Table 11, 26, 127, 128, 134, 155, 156, 171
Talking 48, 160
Trust 47, 50, 72, 146, 148
Truth 22, 25, 32, 34, 36, 44, 47, 49, 50, 52, 65, 68, 78, 117, 120, 128, 146, 162

U

Ultimatums 121, 144, 145
Undercooked food 126
Ungiving 29, 30, 31, 33
Unwrapping 116, 118, 119, 171

W

Withholding sex 145

Other Projects by Anthony C. Rucker aka Da Boogie Man

The Poet, written and experienced
The Poet, the cd
I Can't Believe It's Not Butta
Gabriel's Song
A Word is Worth a Thousand Pictures

Forthcoming titles include…
The Relationship Cookbook Companion Journal
Putting Away Childish Things: The Black Man's Guide to Himself
Daniel: Christian's Living Applications Guide
How to Get HIM Excited About the Wedding
The Lexicon of Loss and Slavery

Visit **relationshipcookbook.com** for more details.

www.ingramcontent.com/pod-product-compliance
Lightning Source LLC
Chambersburg PA
CBHW022104160426
43198CB00008B/342